The First Year at University

WITHDRAWN

D1340609

SRHE and Open University Press Imprint

Helping Students to Learn Series

Series Editor: Rowena Murray

If academics are genuinely to develop as teachers throughout their careers, if they are to continue to produce innovations, they have to bring a scholarly orientation to teaching. This series will show them how to do that. It will teach them how to make credible cases for different forms of innovation, thus helping them to situate teaching centrally in their careers. It will also show them ways of solving students' problems and methods of helping their students to learn more effectively.

Rowena Murray: The Scholarship of Teaching and Learning in Higher Education

Bill Johnston, *The First Year at University: Teaching Students in Transition*

The First Year at University: Teaching Students in Transition

Bill Johnston

Mc Graw Hill

Society for Research into Higher Education
& Open University Press

Open University Press
McGraw-Hill Education
McGraw-Hill House
Shoppenhangers Road
Maidenhead
Berkshire
England
SL6 2QL

email: enquiries@openup.co.uk
world wide web: www.openup.co.uk

and Two Penn Plaza, New York, NY 10121—2289, USA

A catalogue record of this book is available from the British Library

ISBN-13: 978-0-33-523451-6 (pb) 978-0-33-523450-9 (hb)
ISBN-10: 0-33-523451-8 (pb) 0-33-523450-X (hb)

Typeset by Kerrypress, Luton, Bedfordshire
Printed in the UK by Bell and Bain Ltd, Glasgow

Mixed Sources
Product group from well-managed forests and other controlled sources
www.fsc.org   Cert no. TT-COC-002769
© 1996 Forest Stewardship Council
FSC

The McGraw·Hill Companies

CONTENTS

Preface

Why study the first year experience?

Higher education has been traditionally defined by breadth of academic discipline and depth of study. The demands of mass higher education have highlighted other aspects of the curriculum, such as the first year experience (FYE). As a consequence we need to revise our views of the part first year plays in a degree programme and renew our approach to first year teaching and student support. The vision of the first year experience at university in this book is very straightforward. Universities need to offer students a first year wherein their learning experiences:

- meet expectations, engage interest and encourage high standards of effort and achievement;
- empower them for participation in study, employment and lifelong learning.

Universities need to offer this in order to improve the quality of higher education in a mass enrolment system. The challenges are perhaps most acutely felt in first year classes, where large numbers are an issue, and transition experiences can be make or break for some students. For others a successful transition can be the difference between a good degree and a weak one. Universities also need to keep up with each other in terms of good practice and demonstrate that they are adapting to modern conditions. In essence the first year is a major part of every undergraduate's experience and deserves serious attention in every university.

These are key indicators of educational quality, competitiveness and fitness for purpose in the twenty-first century. To do all this I believe universities need to be able to represent honestly to students the importance attached to first year, and the high degree of effort put into making it a successful transition experience. They need to channel that representation through all the interfaces they have with students and their families. These are basic business processes, and should be done well, taking advantage of relevant new technologies to do so.

Even more crucial is how the university represents the importance attached to high quality teaching, feedback and assessment in first year classes. *In this area the representation must align with reality.* It is no good extolling, or even relying on, the institution's reputation, if first year students find staff attitudes and abilities wanting, facilities poor, and the academic challenge uninspiring. In addition, in a mass system, driven by state, employer and student demands for relevance to the job market, it is not enough to show how well the academic disciplines are taught in first year. There must also be a convincing narrative of key skills, graduate attributes and employability. I believe that a story should also be told of the critical importance of higher education for citizenship in a complex and dangerous world.

A first year which meets these criteria will be a powerful formative experience within the degree, leading to better performance and increased satisfaction with choice of university and degree. Such a first year will be the opposite of a transitional period where students are confused about procedures, anxious about fitting in, uncertain about what is expected of them, or how well they are doing, and generally dissatisfied with study and university. Is this too much to ask? If your first reaction is 'yes', then consider the following questions.

- How many students are admitted to first year in your university?

If the answer is in the thousands, which is likely, then consider the sheer volume of human traffic involved, and the scale of infrastructure and resource. Consider also the amount of funding these numbers represent in fees, and consider the financial consequences of every 1 per cent of that funding which might be lost at the end of the year and not replaced for subsequent years.

The 'first year class' is not simply a cash cow, or an undifferentiated mass of stereotypical 'freshers'. Each new cohort brings many of the same transition issues as their predecessors. So the pedagogical and social challenge of first year study has to be renewed and energized every year. This is a task worthy of the best efforts of university teachers and institutional leaders.

- How many students does your department need to 'retain' from first year to second in order to feed a strong honours year?

If the target is not being met, then questions of viability will follow. If the target is being met, indeed if you can afford to impose a quota on numbers, well and good. But what happens if there is a deterioration? Perhaps student interests shift, and they are wooed away to other options. A dip in first to second year retention will have knock-on impact through to honours. If not reversed quickly, this could lead to sharp questions about departmental performance and longer term concerns about programme viability.

- How many students perform to their full potential in first year?

If first year students only get through with bare passes, or an unevenly distributed performance, this may indicate a number of unwelcome issues. For example: fragile selection decisions; a fall-off from school performance; demotivation during first year; failure to adopt effective approaches to study, and many more. A simple majority of students passing should not be accepted as a sufficient benchmark of the educational health of any first year class.

- How much resource is invested in the FYE?

When the preceding points are taken in combination with the practical issues of registration, orientation, timetabling, room allocation, IT provision, staffing, problem solving, gathering student feedback etc. required to make first year work, year after year, it is very clear that first year curriculum should command at least as much attention and resource as other major aspects of university activity.

Enhancing first year in practice

Achieving good practice will not be easy in many cases, nor will it be the result of applying rigid, one-size-fits-all formulae. The pedagogical forms and support mechanisms needed to enhance the first year are contextual, and will of necessity vary between institutions, disciplines and courses. However, the key to enhancement lies within the power of universities, if they can convince academic staff of the need to take first year more seriously as a challenge to their abilities as career educators. Making that case will involve:

- paying more attention to the literature of the FYE;
- raising the status of first year teaching and student support;
- trying out new forms of course organization and adapting teaching to transition;
- rethinking the management of student recruitment, retention and progression as interrelated academic practices and business processes;
- raising the strategic priority attached to the first year, and possibly redeploying resources accordingly.

In short, the FYE and transition should be treated as a key priority of academic policy and business strategy. These are all matters which will be discussed in this book.

If your institution already meets most of the points I have raised, then I hope you will read this book with a colleague's eye and share your insights in the future. On the other hand, if your institution has some way to go with all or some of the points, then I hope you will read on with a view to adapting my thoughts to your circumstances.

Aims of this book

- To build lecturer capacity to understand and influence the first year by making informed decisions on pedagogy
- To augment the lecturer's personal theory of teaching and learning (including reference to the 'folk knowledge' of the department and/or discipline) through discussion of relevant selected literature
- To encourage lecturer resilience and persistence in the face of difficult contexts or problems, and prompt consideration of these in relation to relevant institutional management levels, including strategic, faculty, department and course unit
- To advocate an effective balance of pedagogical activity and student support
- To discuss relevant constructs: 'expectations', 'experience', 'engagement', 'empowerment', 'transition', 'personal development' and 'retention' as foci for innovation
- To summarize and challenge some of the literature on the first year, as a critical guide to lecturers' options for assisting students in first year

These aims will be explored by treating transition and learning in first year as practical issues in the design of courses, teaching and assessment. Consequently, strategies which academics can introduce and evaluate in their classes will be a major focus. In addition, there will be an emphasis on developing teamwork among lecturers in order to spread the load and maximize the impact and consistency of the strategies adopted.

However, given the complexity of the first year, and the growing institutional interest in enhancing student experience, approaches to meeting the needs of different student populations, co-operation between various staff groups and institutional strategic planning will also be discussed.

In dealing with these topics I will draw on my experience and knowledge to combine institutional strategy and operational practice, in relation to institutional contexts and disciplinary cultures. I will propose ways in which lecturers can bring about change systematically and avoid being overburdened with work in the process.

Bill Johnston

Glasgow, 2009

Acknowledgements

For the encouragement to write this book and the advice on how to improve the writing, I am indebted to my colleague and friend, Dr Rowena Murray.

I am also grateful for years of engagement and discussion regarding the first year experience, to many colleagues in Australia, New Zealand, Britain and the USA, especially: Professor Kerri-Lee Krause, Professor Sally Kift, Dr Duncan Nulty, Associate Professor Karen Nelson, Professor Noel Meyers, Dr Judy Skene, Ms Varvara Richards, Dr Wayne Clark, Professor Mantz Yorke and Professor Vincent Tinto.

In Scotland I would like to acknowledge the colleagues who took part in the QAA First Year Enhancement Theme with me, in particular: Ms Rowena Kochanowska, Dr Christine Macpherson, Ms Ruth Whittaker, Dr Ginny Saich, Dr Jonathon Weyers, Professor Ron Piper and Professor Terry Mayes.

For many years of confidences and contributions in the specialist area of Information Literacy I must thank: Ms Sheila Webber, Professor Christine Bruce, Dr Mandy Lupton, Associate Professor Sylvia Edwards, Ms Judy Peacock, Dr Kristina Tovote, Dr Patricia Senn Breivik and Mr Stuart Boon.

My colleagues in the Centre for Academic Practice and Learning Enhancement at the University of Strathclyde should not escape mention, given their many contributions to my ideas on educational development, and their unfailing commitment to keeping my feet on the ground. To that end I would like to acknowledge: Professor George Gordon, Professor David Nicol, Professor Ray Land, Dr Christine Sinclair and Mrs Aileen Wilson. Professor Kenny Miller and Mrs Anne Hughes, Vice and Deputy Principals respectively at Strathclyde, both deserve note for their strong commitment to educational enhancement and student support at the University and more widely in the higher education community. A special acknowledgement must go to my colleague Dr Rebecca Soden, Reader in Education at Strathclyde, for many years of discussion on the nature and practice of academic staff development.

Finally, no book concerning students, learning and teaching should omit mention of the many students who have shared their learning experiences with me over the years. I would like to acknowledge the many hundreds of undergraduates, mainly from Strathclyde University, who have contributed to my understanding over the last twenty years. I would also like to acknowledge several students in particular: Ms Katy McClosky, past President of the University of Strathclyde Students' Association; Mr Tim Cobbett, University of Edinburgh; Mr Gurjit Singh, former President of the National Union of Students Scotland and Ms Rikki Mawad, past President of the University of Tasmania Student Union, who have all taken a particular interest in the first year experience and added to my understanding of the student perspective.

1

First year in a mass higher education system

First year at university: tradition and change

Every year thousands of young people end their schooldays and take stock of the future. Where am I now, where am I going, what has my schooling prepared me to do? Higher education has been an answer to these questions for generations, although it was traditionally an elite choice based on high academic achievement at school. Government interventions in the second half of the twentieth century extended the choice to larger numbers, more mature entrants and a wider range of backgrounds, in a greater variety of institutions. This historical trend was seen as fundamental to the economic and social well-being of all the developed nations, and a cornerstone in building the knowledge-based economy of the twenty-first century. The broad educational response to these conditions, of which higher education is a vital part, is often described using the term *lifelong learning* (Candy *et al.*, 1994; Holford *et al.*, 1998; Dunne, 1999; Istance *et al.*, 2002; Scottish Executive, 2003a, b).

In 2010 we are some thirty-five years down the road of expansion and diversification of tertiary level study described as 'mass' higher education. Martin Trow's perceptive (1974) vision of mass and universal higher education predicted a shift away from an academy serving the needs of an elite of 'bright' school-leavers from families with a tradition of university entrance, and laying claim to professional careers almost as of right. In the future there would be many more students from more diverse backgrounds, entering by a variety of routes to seek the benefits of a degree, and their rates of drop-out would be higher.

Teaching methods would also change in line with the new expanded and diverse student population. The primacy of highly structured degree programmes, small class sizes and collegiality associated with elite higher education would be challenged. In their place Trow envisioned a new world of mass or universal higher education shaped by modularization of courses and formal teaching in large classes, with seminar style teaching conducted by postgraduate teaching assistants. This trend has been observed around the world and provides the educational and organizational context for this examination of the first year experience (FYE hereafter) and student transition. Chapters 2, 3 and 4 of this book will consider the developments in pedagogical thinking in higher education since Trow's paper appeared, and I will explore the organizational implications in Chapter 5.

Whilst the size, shape and contours of higher education have altered greatly, the actual student experience retains many features which would be recognizable to graduates from the start of the twentieth century. Entering first year is one of the most powerful elements of the university experience, representing the beginning of a key period of change in an individual's social life and intellectual development. This period of transformation is often conveyed through notions of 'freshers' being inducted into the norms and practices of the university's undergraduate culture. The resulting patterns of formal acceptance, registration, meeting new friends, confusion, change and frantic socializing, leading to 'exam cramming', eventual graduation and career success, have been portrayed in literature, the cinema and the press, becoming one of the main, popular motifs of university life in western culture.

My favourite popular example is in the film *Chariots of Fire*, celebrating the Olympic Games which took place in Paris after the end of the First World War. The main characters are Cambridge undergraduates, who are introduced through their engagement with the equivalent of freshers' week, in that noble institution circa 1919. The opening scenes are shaped by the clamour of the 'clubs and societies fayre'. Athletics, naturally, but also the Gilbert and Sullivan Society, and the staple groupings of 'student politics'. Understandably in this case, pacifism and socialism jousted with the traditional parties of government, to claim the allegiance of a post-war generation of students. Later in the narrative, one of the main characters from outside the Oxbridge circle, Eric Liddell, the Scots Olympic medallist, is shown pursuing his studies at the University of Edinburgh, in the daunting shadow of John Knox, as preparation for missionary work in China.

Although the focus of the film is on ambition and athletic excellence, the ancient universities and their traditions are a potent force in conveying the spirit of the times, providing the immediate social context for the athletes. The dominant social images for me are of privilege, empire and nationalism. The undergraduates are clearly of the privileged class, embracing a traditional higher education. That elite education is as much a part of the nation's establishment as the British Olympic Committee of the day, led by the Prince of Wales and composed of the great and the good of a previous generation of public school and elite university men. Competing with other nations and beating them to the medals is a dominant theme of the pursuit of excellence for this group in its time.

There are dark sides to this world, for example the casual anti-Semitism of the College Masters in their attitude to Harold Abrams, the gold medallist, whose absolute determination to win and beat the establishment at their own games they dismiss as vulgar. His passion is at odds with the traditional account of excellence, both academic and athletic, achieved through a graceful amateurism born out of 'good breeding'. In a different social and national register, Eric Liddell's decision not to compete on a Sunday, in deference to his religious beliefs, is incomprehensible to a British Olympic Committee, who cannot accept that religious conviction might overcome allegiance to king and country, when national pride in competition is at stake. To this sub-cast of the British establishment of the time, Liddell must have seemed like the archetypal 'uncompromising Scot', just as Abrams must have appeared as the stereotypical 'wealthy and ambitious Jew' pushing his way up the social ladder.

My own freshers' week at the end of the 1960s, at a strongly scientific and technological university in a great nineteenth-century industrial city, did not have the dinner jackets and college scarves of the past. However, we did have the club and society stalls at registration, complete with Sports Union and political groups – CND and Anti-Apartheid being prominent. Images of the recent student revolts in continental Europe were also much in evidence. Had I been transported back to that Cambridge freshers' week of 1919 as portrayed in *Chariots of Fire*, I would have immediately understood what was going on.

The point, of course, is that coming to university has always been a mixture of educational, social, imaginative and cultural experiences, grounded and shaped by specific institutional forms of induction and socialization. Practical questions of prior educational experience, prerequisite knowledge, attitude and skill determine university entrance, and to some extent set agendas for transition. Equally, the answers to these questions can illuminate the inequalities and opportunities represented by society's wider schooling systems and political priorities.

First year experiences are varied, therefore, and it may be better to think in terms of 'multiple first years', with nuanced transitions influenced by diverse backgrounds and contexts, rather than a unified one-size-fits-all format. To that extent the term FYE is perhaps best seen as a helpful shorthand for a complex and dynamic reality.

Why work on developing the FYE?

Whilst each individual who has experienced university will have her or his own memories and perceptions of first year transitions, and these may be very powerful influences in their lives, that alone should not be the primary warrant for careful study of the FYE. There are compelling academic and institutional reasons for action. Whittaker (2008) has summarized the fundamental arguments well:

> Approaches to supporting transition are linked to: improving preparedness for HE; easing integration into the university environment, both

academically and socially; and encouraging the development of the independent learner. By shifting the focus of transition from student retention and withdrawal to supporting the engagement and empowerment of all students, successful transition can be measured not simply in terms of whether students continue on their programmes, but whether in doing so they are provided with the opportunity to achieve their full potential.

To this first year transition agenda might be added:

• issues of wider access and diversity in the student population;
• student life–work balance and the financial context for student support;
• demands for greater attention to student 'employability' in the curriculum;
• information culture, the related technologies and the internet.

Institutions therefore need to recognize that the way students experience transition influences persistence, retention and success, and they should respond by prioritizing systematic efforts to scaffold transition in first year with specific pedagogical and support measures.

These matters are discussed in this book in relation to relevant literature, enhancements in pedagogy and curriculum, and with an emphasis on the organizational challenges involved. The rest of this introduction will develop answers to my 'why work on the FYE?' question and thereby set out the background to such work under the following headings:

• Transition: concepts, issues and support
• Students and study: academic and social transitions
• Diversity: cultural transitions
• The first year reviewed: a new institutional approach
• Implications for lecturers: pedagogy and career development

Transition

At this point it will be helpful to consider the term transition in more detail to illuminate how it is deployed in the FYE discourse. Transition can be described as a double-sided concept comprising:

• the student experience of change involved in joining the university;
• the programmes of academic and other activities, which the university provides to support and enhance student transition.

The changes invoked can include leaving school/college etc., moving to a new place, meeting new people and taking on a new set of financial obligations. Transition can occur in different dimensions – academic, personal, financial, social etc., and students who manage one aspect may struggle in another.

Transition issues

These encompass any aspect of student FYE which requires a change of perspective and action by an individual in order to appreciate the new situation, settle into the new environment, meet requirements, fulfil expectations, overcome setbacks, take advantage of opportunities and otherwise achieve success. For example:

- **Cultural and community changes:** move from school/college to university; move from familiar social class, ethnic, religious affiliations, and regional locations; diverse levels of cultural capital in relation to the institution, its staff and student peers; linguistic differences
- **Academic changes:** encounters with new subjects and concepts of learning; increased quantity of material and tasks; different approaches to teaching and learning from school; differing academic writing conventions; analytical approach to subjects; requirement for increased self-regulation of effort and time on task; responsibility for safe working practice in laboratories; team work and projects; new feedback and assessment practices
- **Social changes:** anonymity of large classes; new town; separation from friends and family; living in halls of residence; meeting people from very different backgrounds and people with very different values and attitudes; so-called 'non-traditional' experiences
- **Personal changes:** developing realistic self-assessment; accepting and enjoying intellectually challenging tasks; adapting strategies for managing disability; confronting employment and financial imperatives; commuting; career aspiration/indecision; stress tolerance

Transition not only affects students entering the first year of a course. Direct entrants to later years experience a similar range of issues and need the same level of provision. There is also the issue of transition from first year to second year, in terms of options to revise academic and career choices and opportunities to anticipate the experience of new challenges in teaching and learning. The year 1–2 transition can be a major time for reorientations in outlook, ambitions and approaches; it can also be a time of disengagement and motivational 'slump'.

Support for transition

Effective transition activities may be both informal in nature and part of formal structures devised by the university to support positive first year experiences. All approaches address the obvious fact that students take time to adjust to the university and adapt to academic rigour in their disciplines.

Effective activities should also reflect the diverse and changing social and educational needs and experiences of first year students.

Students and study: academic and social transition across the generations

Whilst it might be attractive to assume that university entrants come to university more or less ready-made with all the attitudes and skills required for study, massification has doused such rose-tinted assumptions in very cold water. Underfunded increases in student numbers, wider access and greater diversity combine in many instances to sharpen the need for assistance with transition to university. However, despite the need for more attention to transition, the institutional response is often muted, and over-reliant on piecemeal and reactive measures to specific problems and crises. Perennially low in status, first year teaching has not enjoyed the rate of systematic pedagogical change it deserves, thereby leaving the FYE marooned between general introductory advice and support programmes and the mainstream of teaching.

In essence the concern now is that more students are entering higher education lacking academic skills and attitudes previously regarded as basic to tertiary level work, which is leading to uncertainty, disengagement and cynicism about the traditional values of university study (Yorke, 1999; Biggs, 2007). Concern is often linked to institutional and governmental worries about student retention rates and doubts regarding the effectiveness of wider access policies. The traditional response to transition assumed that such problems were the preserve of a minority of 'at risk' students, and could be addressed by specific measures targeted at them. Providing support could therefore be left to a few concerned academics backed by central support services, with relatively limited resources to back their commitment. This response is looking increasingly out of date and unfit for purpose in twenty-first-century mass higher education, hence the pressing need to renew the first year curriculum and adapt pedagogy to meet the needs of students in transition.

Employability

Allied to this scenario for academic change is the vastly increased demand for higher education to be economically relevant, and in particular for degrees to develop specific employment-related skills in addition to teaching knowledge of academic disciplines. The policy context for UK higher education has been dominated by the OECD agenda of knowledge economy, global competitiveness, technological change and inclusive lifelong learning as key policy imperatives for national competitiveness and prosperity. This vision has remained consistent through the decades of Conservative administration at the end of the twentieth century, and the post-millennium New Labour administrations in the UK. In essence the notion of education developing the human capital for economic growth provides the dominant perspective, shaping policy and influencing pedagogy in higher education.

The construct *employability* (Higher Education Funding Council for England, 2003; Denholm *et al.*, 2003; Knight and Yorke, 2003) is a current focus of the human capital perspective in course design and teaching practice in the UK. Employability may have features in common with the Australian notion of 'work readiness' as an objective of undergraduate education and an emerging, evidence-based measure of quality.

The 'net generation' of students

In addition to the concerns detailed above, there has been a growth in 'generational' descriptions of the student body. Terms such as 'net generation' (Tapscott, 1999) and 'digital natives' (Prensky, 2001, 2005) have emerged to describe the generation born between 1984 and 1994. This generation is portrayed as being immersed in the new digital technologies, connected to each other via the internet and their mobile phones, preferring these modes of communication and information gathering to traditional print-based modes. Howe and Strauss (2000, 2003) round out the picture somewhat, applying the term 'millennials' to indicate their potentially key roles in future society, and suggest a qualitative difference from pre-digital experience in terms of their approaches to communication, learning and socialization.

As a consequence of these related aspects of the student relationship to the FYE, institutions have begun to pay greater attention to the ways students are inducted into academic study and a variety of initiatives have been developed. In essence, older terms like study skills are being revised and updated to take account of the new requirements of study in a digital environment, and to develop the 'key skills' or 'graduate attributes' deemed essential to the modern graduate labour markets.

Diversity: cultural transitions

The student body of the early twenty-first century is likely to be diverse and complex in a variety of ways, and institutions need to renew their approach to transition to reflect this. At the most basic level, the plethora of equal opportunities legislation requiring formal systems to ensure compliance sheds light on some aspects of diverse populations. Candidate groups would include:

- first generation students;
- ethnic groups;
- gay, lesbian, bisexual and transgender students;
- migrants;
- students with disabilities.

Typical responses by institutions involve promulgating policy for:

- meeting multicultural needs;
- recognizing intercultural communication and learning styles;
- enhancing preparation and transition for target population members;
- generally supporting 'non-traditional' students.

Initiatives to deliver such policies include:

- appointing dedicated staff;
- introducing specific course units on diversity;
- providing targeted programmes;
- sensitization training;
- curriculum revision for learner empowerment.

Whilst the need to comply with legislation has placed diversity firmly on the agenda, we should look beyond that stage and consider how to harness the diverse experiences and ambitions of students. As first year classes come to reflect more closely the diversity of the wider society and economy, we should devise ways to use the raw material of diverse experience whenever possible to engage and empower students. A focus on diversity also takes the debate beyond the objectives of 'newcomers' becoming accustomed to the academy's ways of teaching and learning, and raises subtle questions of identity and acculturation, which require research to inform and improve practice.

The first year reviewed: a new institutional approach

I suggest that the preceding factors, which have grown in significance in recent decades, require a new institutional approach that significantly uplifts the status of work on the FYE, particularly in relation to academic contributions and career progression of lecturers. Responses and measures for the FYE should not, therefore, be confined to the central support services in universities, or the contributions of a few particularly engaged academics. There should be greater responsibility on all academics as teachers, course co-ordinators and policy makers, thereby raising the status and priority attached to first year teaching as a mainstream academic activity. I will explore this perspective in detail in Chapters 2, 3 and 4.

In addition, I will discuss the need for institutional policy and management to prize FYE activities as highly as other core activities of research and resource management (Chapter 5).

My vision of this new institutional approach includes:

- placing far greater emphasis on first year teaching and accepting first year teaching as a specialized academic activity;
- taking greater account of student experiences and developing greater student–staff dialogue;
- redesigning first year classes and rearticulating whole degree programmes;
- reviewing institutional culture, structures and priorities to better support FYE.

How this approach can be implemented, and why it is important, will be the pervasive themes of this book. I will illuminate the themes by identifying relevant ideas from literature and practice (Chapter 2), relating them to pedagogical practice (Chapters 3 and 4), and arguing for an uplift in the institutional priority given to the FYE in Chapter 5.

Analytical perspectives on a renewed FYE

The fact that I have more than one objective in writing about the FYE makes it more complex than it would be if I were focused solely on questions of teaching practice for example, with little reference to pedagogical innovation and institutional change. Consequently it is important at this stage to suggest an analytical framework for my examination of the FYE. The framework I will use to examine the FYE and develop my perspective on the new institutional approach comprises two interrelated ways of looking at the FYE:

- First: *the institutional context of the FYE*, described by the institutional responses and measures adopted to support student transition and engagement with the experience of high quality learning
- Secondly: *the macro context of the FYE*, described as the foundational part of a degree programme in a mass or universal higher education system, comprising increased numbers and greater diversity of intake, strongly influenced by demands for economic relevance, and facing a rapidly changing economic outlook for graduates

Whilst the bulk of this book is concerned with the first perspective, the second is equally important.

Institutional context: realities and strategic choices

This is the first category of my analytical framework. This frame addresses the FYE in the context of overall institutional mission and management, with an emphasis on the daily realities of teaching, learning and student support. In other words, it acknowledges that specific responses and measures for FYE and transition are part of the wider institutional agenda of academic strategy and competing resource priorities.

In the past, it is likely that the FYE received relatively limited attention in the deliberations of institutional managers and academic committees. However, massification and the influence of external quality assessment have all raised the profile of work on FYE, particularly in relation to measures to improve transition and induce student satisfaction with their experience. Allied to these influences are concerns with retention, and the need to comply with legal obligations in respect of diversity, equality and students with special needs.

Understandably this has led institutions to focus on strategic responses to mitigate any negative fallout from increased numbers and wider access. The FYE has therefore begun to feature in institutional discussions of academic strategy at university, faculty and departmental levels. Whilst much of this discussion is likely to be conducted at committees of Senate, and perhaps also strategic management bodies, it is also a concern for new, as well as experienced lecturers, who, even if they do not teach first years themselves, will encounter former first year students at some point in their undergraduate teaching. At that point they will discover whether or not the experiences those students had in first year prove to be a suitable baseline for their own teaching.

Complexity of first year experience and stakeholder differences

I will summarize a number of fundamental insights into the complexity of FYE as an institutional issue. The FYE presents in a range of forms in different institutional contexts:

- item of policy analysis and strategic planning;
- unit of organizational and management responsibility;
- constituent part of academic strategy and practice;
- concrete approaches and measures to support student transition;
- tangible experiences of students coming into first year.

A key question is to determine how integrated and aligned these various forms are in your institution, and what factors influence the degree of coherence between policy and practice.

The decisive factor at present, I believe, is the existence of significant, often competing differences in stakeholder assumptions about, and perceptions of, FYE, with an associated absence of a specific, unifying institutional locus for responsibility and action. For example:

- Senior officers emphasize notional costs, statistical returns and national league tables, whilst faculty/departmental interest tends much more towards local student numbers, retention and pass rates
- Student Services and Student Unions strongly emphasize student well-being, advocacy and support; this approach is shared by many academics, whilst counterpointed by their concern for academic rigour and standards, and the long-term viability of their courses
- A common institutional management tendency is to overemphasize retention problems, and attribute concerns to particular departments/ courses, or factors such as lower entry level standards, poor monitoring of progress, ineffective pastoral care etc.

These differences are spread over various, sometimes competing, levels of institutional organization, and this makes it very difficult to establish institutional consensus about priorities, practices and the means to bring about improvements. In particular it can be very difficult for individual lecturers to see where institutional priorities lie, and to decide their commitments accordingly.

Macro context: human capital and the graduate society

Whilst state and sector interest in human capital accounts of higher education persists as the defining influence on the context of higher education (HE), it is evident that numbers will be increased where possible, and that employability will gain force as an influence on curriculum and course design (Teichler, 1999). Under such conditions, higher education has come to be described with a strong emphasis on the preparation of graduates for work in an information-rich, knowledge-based economy (Arnold, 1997; Elias and Purcell, 2001; King, 2003; Australian Government, Department of Education, Science and Training, 2004).

Whilst it is arguable that making direct connections between levels of education and increased economic growth is naïve, and underplays the many other factors influencing the economy (Wolf, 2002), it is undeniable that state interest in developing the nation's 'human capital' has been decisive in the unprecedented growth in higher education at the end of the twentieth century. Acknowledging this powerful influence does not, however, devalue the views of those who emphasize the traditional role of universities as havens of investigation, explanation and social critique, rather than as simple tools of economic policy (Taylor *et al.*, 2002).

Central to this macro level of description must be a recognition that preparing students for the world of work after graduation, by developing graduates who are self-aware learners and reflective professionals, is now a key responsibility for higher education. Terms such as 'key skills', 'graduate attributes', 'employability' and 'work readiness' have come into common usage to identify desirable characteristics of graduates (Harvey *et al.*, 1997; Drew, 1998; Bennet *et al.*, 2000; Symes and McIntyre, 2000; Knight and Yorke, 2003; Hawkridge, 2005). Teaching such attributes also implies skill development linked to modern recruitment practices and recognition that organizations are significant sites of learning, and continuing professional development (Sparrow, 1997; Anderson and Ostroff, 1997; Stewart and Knowles, 2000; Bennet *et al.*, 2000; King, 2003; Mayrhofer *et al.*, 2005; Searle, 2005).

These trends should, of course, be balanced by research which challenges the more visionary accounts of working life in the new knowledge economy, and draws attention to more critical accounts of the nature of job markets and the organization of work (du Gay, 1996; Thompson and Warhurst, 1998; Moynagh and Worsley, 2005; Baldry *et al.*, 2007). The tension between these differing perspectives is likely to gain added force as the causes and consequences of the 2008 credit crisis, and the ensuing global recession, become clearer.

This state of affairs has implications for FYE, in terms of how courses are described to incoming students, how those students' transition to university is managed and how they are taught and assessed. The task, in short, is to educate students who are capable of continuing to learn after they have graduated – albeit with a focus on the workplace: a task which chimes with public policy for lifelong learning.

Lifelong learning in a graduate society

Regardless of the actual impact the human capital approach may have on national competitiveness, it is very likely to ensure that the generations who came into the mass higher education systems in the 1980s and afterwards will form a significant section of the population in OECD countries at least, by 2020 and beyond. It is arguable that the ideal of lifelong learning may be achieved through their values, their approach to their children's education, their influence on government and their sheer length of life expectancy. A key question for the future can be framed in terms of the extent to which universities have developed a pedagogy which is congruent with the characteristics that support learning throughout life. The part the FYE has in that development is obviously an important strand running through this book and I will return to it in the concluding chapter.

Implications for lecturers

At this point it is necessary to focus all of the foregoing ideas on the role of the lecturer as a key resource in enhancing the FYE. I will summarize this notion in two sections:

- FYE and pedagogy;
- career development.

FYE and pedagogy: lecturers' daily lives

From a lecturer's point of view all the strands outlined above may be experienced as an underfunded increase in undergraduate class sizes and marking workloads, with more diverse cohorts adding to their workload difficulties. Additionally, many lecturers are expected to perform other functions, principally research and postgraduate supervision. Reduced time for these activities can undermine their career prospects and institutional income from research and postgraduate sources.

As the traditional emphasis on subject teaching by formal lectures and examinations is under pressure of change in response to new student expectations and patterns of engagement, and also as a consequence of new technologies, workloads may increase. Finally, the influence of external quality assurance procedures, and increasingly sharp demands that universities prepare students with skill sets closely aligned to employer needs for flexibility, team working, entrepreneurial attitudes and so forth, must also be taken into account. This is a demanding agenda for an experienced academic, let alone a recently appointed probationer, since it impacts the broad features of academic employment, and also specific issues related to teaching workload.

All of these factors have direct relevance to the FYE in terms of student expectations and experience, and the responses and measures taken by universities to manage and enhance first year. In short, student transition and engagement cannot be left to chance, but require systematic action at all levels of the institution in order to maximize successful first year experiences, which lay the foundation for subsequent study. Lecturers are key to such action, so it is critical that they reflect on teaching first year students as a distinctive group, considering their particular needs and devising an approach aligned to those needs.

Why should lecturers bother developing the FYE?

In extremis, problems of student recruitment/retention can threaten the stability of courses and the job security of staff. Poor student satisfaction ratings in local and national surveys can question quality of provision, damage reputations and perhaps depress recruitment. On a more positive note, I suggest that lecturers can benefit academically and personally from teaching which helps students to be more effective learners and engages students with their disciplines – in effect, teaching which is more enjoyable and satisfying, and which is regularly renewed and not simply 'reviewed' as an administrative chore. These are substantial matters and will be explored in Chapters 3, 4, and 5; however, for the present let us consider some basic points suggesting what universities might do to help lecturers enhance their first year teaching.

Career development and the status of first year teaching: how can we help lecturers?

It is my contention that the FYE and transition are fundamental to educational experience, and therefore a core responsibility of the academic community. I shall develop this claim throughout the book by considering what can be done in practice to develop teaching, assessment and course design to enhance the FYE. However, I do not attempt this purely as an exercise in exhorting hard-pressed lecturers to 'do more' within existing resources and structures. I believe that what is needed is an institutional commitment to reward staff for building a career in teaching, with the FYE as one of a number of specialist strands. Equally, there may also be a case for institutions to consider a redistribution of resources to FYE activities from later years of study, and perhaps from other activities, to align with FYE enhancement.

The focus must be on the implications for lecturers' practice and professional development as educators, allied to the nature of institutional support for such activities. Career development in relation to FYE activity is firmly within this context. I treat these matters as issues in the long-term development of career academics, who will necessarily have to manage their careers in teaching, research, university administration and community service over several decades. Therefore time spent on the task of understanding the FYE is time well spent, not only as a way to make teaching first years more effective and enjoyable, but as a cornerstone in developing academic leadership potential. If you can build a professorial career by disciplinary specialism and research, why not build a career on teaching specialism? Achieving this goal would require at the very least:

- adopting a critical approach informed by learning principles;
- prioritizing student transition;
- demonstrating knowledge of theory and research on teaching and learning, to underpin choice of teaching methods and assessment practices.

To support such career mindfullness I have devised a simple model of the components of career development which can be conceived of as a cyclic, iterative process. This model can be displayed in a linear form and mapped roughly against the chapters in this book:

- Developing an awareness of the importance of the FYE to the university – Chapters 1 and 2
- Accessing relevant literature and gaining an overall perspective – Chapters 2 and 3
- Deciding on teaching strategies and reflecting on practice – Chapters 3 and 4
- Working in terms of institutional strategy – Chapter 5
- Synthesizing knowledge and experience as part of a mature professionalism – Chapter 6

In subsequent chapters I will suggest some practical exercises and activities to support the various stages of this model. For example, 'What would you do if you had to …

- teach a large first year biomedical course;
- with a high intake of non-native English speakers;
- a varied science education background across the whole class;

and you were a lecturer in …

- an elite university with an international reputation?'

As we go on I will address problems like this by applying some key concepts in the FYE literature and exploring a variety of teaching strategies and their implementation, in particular how the strategies might vary by discipline, type of institution, nature of the student body and your access to supporting resources. In the meantime see Gleeson *et al.* (www.fyhe.qut.edu.au/past_papers/2006/Nuts%20&%20Bolts/Gleeson.pdf) for a view of how one group of science lecturers tackled the real situation outlined in the scenario. Once you become familiar with this conference website, I'd suggest browsing for papers which fit your own interests. This device is intended to illustrate the FYE as a complex teaching challenge and stimulate proactive, searching strategies as part of academic staff development.

Conclusion

Some at least of the foregoing points are likely to impact every institution and, whilst the impact may vary in degree, there is no denying the increased importance of FYE on institutional agendas. Traditional notions of student 'deficit' and 'drop-out' which may have been adequate in the past cannot survive in the face of increased numbers and greater diversity. The rise of 'employability' and 'graduate attributes' as essential features of degree studies cannot be ignored or downplayed in the face of state policy on economic relevance and lifelong learning

This book describes the main responses to this new situation in HE, as they relate to the FYE. This is presented as a blend of literature, practical exercises and perspectives drawn from practice. The basic flow of argument is to compare possible institutional approaches to the FYE – central service provision, academic mainstreaming, course redesign – and relate this to the need for greater institutional strategic management of FYE. The book concludes by reviewing the prospects for the FYE in the next 5 to 15 years.

This book speaks to lecturers about the teaching challenges called into play by the academic and social adjustments students have to make in first year courses. Other readers (Vice Chancellors and other senior officers; administrators, librarians, information technology specialists and educational developers) should consider how they can best help lecturers and students put the most into the FYE by creating supportive conditions and funding the appropriate infrastructure.

The following chapters will explore these themes and argue a case for change in the way the FYE is conceived and managed by institutions and their staff. A key aim is to suggest powerful connections between the macro world of socio-economic trends, the intermediate world of university strategic management and the micro worlds of teaching, learning and assessment. I believe that making these connections, and encouraging others to make and debate their own connections, is fundamental to changing and enhancing teaching practice and the student experience of first year at university as a significant element of lifelong learning in an information culture.

2

What do we know about teaching first year students, and what should we do with that knowledge?

Introduction

The quick answer to the first question in the chapter title is 'quite a lot'. The knowledge is split between general literature on teaching and learning, which has been developed mainly to explain and guide disciplinary teaching, and more specific literature dealing with the FYE. This latter material entails support mechanisms and structures as well as teaching, to acknowledge the holistic nature of the FYE and the contributions other staff make. As to the second question about what we should do with the knowledge to guide teaching practice, I think the answer is twofold. First, explore the different writers and develop a critical awareness of the strengths, weaknesses and nuances of their positions. Secondly, take some concepts from the literature and apply them to our own teaching practices. This latter activity is absolutely essential and need not be too onerous, as I hope to show at the end of the chapter.

This chapter relates the prospects for first year teaching and learning to a body of professional literature, which lecturers can choose to use as a guide to their daily teaching activities. Reading the literature and trying out the ideas are interdependent activities, and you will get most benefit by treating them as such. Whilst the theoretical material will be presented mainly in the form of a selective discussion of that literature, I want to encourage readers to begin relating ideas from the literature to some relevant themes from the chapter:

- Adopting a critical approach to teaching informed by learning principles

For example, to what extent does the account of teaching, and the FYE, reported in the literature accord with your own experiences? If there are differences, how do you account for them? Does the literature offer new ways of thinking about the FYE and your teaching?

- Prioritizing the FYE in the curriculum

For example, how might you go about getting students to understand academic expectations/conventions and participate more actively in classroom work? How would those desirable outcomes be related to notions about how students learn and gain deeper understanding?

Answers may not leap out from the page immediately, and you may want to follow up on some of the references, and read the full texts, before forming a view. Equally, the practical exercise which concludes the chapter may help navigate these questions and also act as an advance organizer for thinking about the examples and proposals in Chapters 3 and 4. This chapter is therefore a hybrid of literature survey and practical guidance. It is part of a basic 'toolkit' for lecturers who have accepted that the first year is a key stage in a degree programme, and want to respond by improving first year teaching.

If you think of this chapter as a summary of some ideas from the literature to dip into and follow up over time, whilst working with colleagues to build up a practice of peer discussion and observation of teaching, then you will have a clear sense of what I am trying to achieve. As such, this chapter is intended to bridge into Chapter 3, where the combination of conceptual and practical approaches is further developed through case studies and a systematic account of how lecturers might enhance their contributions to first year teaching.

The thematic structure of the chapter is as follows:

- Teaching and educational development
- The literature – development and critique
- Teaching first year students
- Engagement and empowerment – student views
- Concepts into practice – a strategy

Teaching: contexts, constraints and opportunities

Teaching is firmly grounded in decisions about choice of content, and desired outcomes, balanced against the practical constraints imposed by core factors such as class size, available teaching space, timetables, resources and university regulations. The requirements of accrediting bodies, and the more recent demands for broad employability skills, add further complexity to decision making. Institutional concerns to meet state and funding body requirements for quality assurance and enhancement in mass higher education have been paralleled by the growing complexity of university policies and structures for managing academic affairs.

From a lecturer's perspective there is the ever-present tension between time spent on first year teaching, and the relative status attached to this work by the university, against the demands of other academic activities. Decisions about first year teaching can reflect combinations of these constraining factors, which may lead to students being taught 'basic' content, in large classes, with relatively little systematic attention paid to the transition issues described in Chapter 1. This in turn can fuel student dissatisfaction, disengagement and underperformance.

However, the point of teaching is surely to encourage students to enjoy learning about their subjects, to succeed, and to develop analytical, practical, creative and personal abilities in the process. This has always been a given of university teaching in all disciplines, expressed through notions of students becoming independent learners, critical thinkers and more rounded individuals as they become chemists, historians, teachers etc. Teaching at its best should be a source of ideas and questions, not simply a rehearsal of content. Learning, by the same token, should be a product of imagination, invention and expression. We do not always achieve these aims, but they are enduring benchmarks of a university education, and demand our best efforts.

These familiar nostrums describe for me what could be called the native 'guiding theory' of teaching held by many generations of lecturers, and disseminated informally through disciplinary communities and departmental colleagues. It strikes me that in this 'guiding theory' lies an opportunity to enhance first year teaching, through engagement with the relevant literature, modification of teaching practice and active experimentation with new course designs to bring about valued ends. It is this process of making informed decisions and evaluating the experience of teaching in relation to learning which I view as best practice.

First year teaching is a good focus for this approach right across the curriculum, since the sooner students can be encouraged to treat their studies as an exercise in intellectual development, as opposed to simply passing exams, the more likely they are to begin developing the requisite dispositions and approaches deemed appropriate for learning in higher education. Equally, the sooner first year students participate with staff and other students in stimulating learning activities, the sooner they are likely to feel part of the university, and more socially settled in that learning environment.

In the longer term, a challenging first year with good support and feedback should increase the likelihood of academic success and personal development, leading to greater levels of student satisfaction. This is common sense, and the staff effort involved can be considered as an investment, which will pay dividends in the form of increased student engagement and better retention rates.

Educational development, ideals and realities

The more aware teachers are of the accounts of learning identified in the literature, and the variety of teaching and assessment strategies used by other lecturers, the more options they have in deciding their own teaching practices. Thus their 'guiding theory' of teaching, developed in practice and from more experienced colleagues, can be enhanced by engagement with literature, and the result should be better teaching, which in addition is more personally satisfying. What forms might this engagement take? The last decade has seen a move to formalize the 'training' lecturers receive in pedagogy through Graduate Certificates, and a range of other continuing professional development (CPD) initiatives concerned with teaching. Institutions insist that new staff engage with some form of pedagogical development as part of probationary appointment, and encourage ongoing development as well.

It would be naïve to assume that all lecturers wholeheartedly embrace the pedagogical literature and related development opportunities, or that all institutions offer incentives and rewards for teaching on a par with research and other activities. I have spent too many hours debating the value of educational theory for practice, and commiserating with colleagues who feel that teaching is less highly prized than research, to have any shreds of such naïvety left. However, I am constantly encouraged by colleagues who embrace the notion of enhancing their teaching and make the effort to overcome intellectual, practical and institutional barriers.

One such colleague, a professor, eminent in her discipline of management science, and very active in university administration, summed the matter up well. For her it is a case of innovating her teaching practice in order to maintain her motivation, stimulate student interest, and avoid the staleness which can come from overuse of one approach. Another colleague, who worked with me on a two-year project to enhance student critical thinking in his discipline of computer science, described the educational development process to be '... exactly like research' (Gent *et al.*, 1999: 518). By this he meant that changing his teaching entailed the same level of intellectual challenge, frustration and satisfaction as his research activity. Both colleagues display powerful intrinsic motivations related to key aspects of an academic's career – personal satisfaction, student learning and research activity. I believe that, given a choice, most students would vote to be taught by lecturers who approached teaching from positions like those described.

Influence of the literature

In both these cases, discussion and use of pedagogical literature was a prime factor in the experiences the colleagues described. Also, both colleagues were experienced academics with developed research careers, and to that extent are worth taking seriously by new academics, as potential role models. In any case, it is important for newcomers to gain some familiarity with the literature given the current institutional expectation that lecturers will be able to *demonstrate knowledge of theory and research on teaching and learning, to underpin choice of teaching methods and assessment practices.*

The linkage of pedagogical knowledge with institutional concern to ensure academic staff development fits the model of academic teaching career development outlined in Chapter 1 in respect of the 'stages' of:

- accessing relevant literature and gaining an overall perspective;
- deciding on strategies and reflecting on practice.

The application of these ideas from the literature to practice will receive more detailed treatment in Chapters 3 and 4. This account of teaching and learning strategies will underpin and advance the changes in university organization described in Chapter 5.

What do we know about teaching students?

My purpose in this section is briefly to introduce the broad literature on teaching and learning in higher education. Experienced colleagues may be familiar with the general work on student learning and university teaching discussed below. I believe that newcomers are increasingly familiar with the general literature, through their own efforts and the reading lists accompanying Postgraduate Certificate in Education (PGCE) courses that they may be taking. Consequently I will concentrate on simply flagging up some of the main authors and giving my interpretation of the strengths and weaknesses of this body of work. Hopefully my interpretations will open up some new avenues of thought, and stimulate further reading, or rereading of texts, to illuminate practice.

I have organized this section under four main headings:

- Main features of the literature
- Key sources
- Constructive alignment
- Some critiques of this literature

Hopefully this signposting of my thinking will help readers estimate how closely their views align with mine, or perhaps offer some new pathways for reflection.

Main features of the literature: constructivism, the current orthodoxy

The period of massification outlined in Chapter 1 has been paralleled by the growth of a new discourse on teaching, learning and assessment in higher education. Much of the contemporary literature promotes the notion that the more actively engaged students are in their learning the better. This view of learning is encapsulated in the notion of *constructivism*, which indicates that learning is not a simple matter of memorization, but rather a complex intellectual activity of creating deeper meaning and understanding through practical activity, reflection and judgement. Consequently the lecturer's task is portrayed as one of designing learning activities to achieve that end, and encouraging students to adopt a deep approach to learning. Thus lecturers are represented as mediating their subject knowledge by using more involving methods to achieve active student engagement and understanding of the subject. This image is contrasted with methods to simply transmit subject information for students to note or otherwise consume at a relatively superficial level.

In the new discourse, lectures, tutorials and laboratories are conducted more interactively, with more student participation, to develop their understanding and build self-confidence. Group projects are deployed to investigate subject matter, perhaps using real-world problems as a focus, and with clear aims to develop interpersonal and communication skills. Terms like 'reflection', 'self-regulation', 'metacognition' and 'creativity' are now commonly used to characterize learning, and describe some of the day-to-day tasks, activities and processes that students are asked to engage with as part of their courses. The use of online resources is assumed to be ubiquitous, backing up teaching, facilitating communication and channelling students to seek out information for themselves.

Finally, assessment is seen as more of a question of motivating students and providing feedback to improve future performance, and less as a simple matter of judgement and rank marking. Recent National Student Survey (NSS) results in the UK criticizing the quality of assessment and feedback have underlined the importance students place on these activities, and emphasized the need for lecturers and institutions to acknowledge the problem and investigate how best to change their approaches (www.thestudentsurvey.com/). Clearly the reported experience of final year students should give a strong steer to what should be happening from first year onwards.

The implications for the student experience are quite marked. For example, students would spend more time on tasks designed to encourage deeper processing of information and ideas, rather than memorizing and regurgitating content. This would take them beyond lecture notes and library shelves to the online information cornucopia, and require them to select, analyse and apply knowledge to complex problems. This in turn would require developing good knowledge of reliable information sources, allied with the intellectual ability to formulate and refine search strategies, and the searching skills demanded by different databases and web resources. Project work would occupy a greater portion of formal learning and be assessed on a par with paper and pencil-type assessments and examinations.

Students would also be expected to take progressively greater responsibility for their own learning and to collaborate in this with other students on team projects. In time they would be expected to reflect on their development, refine their approaches and build a convincing profile of their abilities to be traded in the graduate job market, offered as evidence of potential for postgraduate study and as a component of their approach to lifelong learning.

Key sources: improving course design, teaching, learning, assessment and feedback

A number of key, current texts which should sit side by side on every lecturer's bookshelves in the section marked 'teaching' are:

- Biggs (2007): combines ideas about student learning and systematic course design in the construct *constructive alignment*. Emphasis on large classes and the demands of mass higher education
- Entwistle and Tomlinson (2007): provides a comprehensive account of the development of ideas about teaching, learning and assessment in higher education over the last thirty years, through chapters by many of the main contributors
- Barnett and Coate (2005): illuminates the idea of curriculum and provides a stimulating counterpoint to Biggs's views on constructive alignment
- Fry *et al.* (2003): provides practical 'how to' guides for a variety of teaching practices, in a series of concise chapters

The key current resource which is specific to assessment and feedback in relation to first year in particular is the Re-engineering Assessment Practice Project website (www.reap.ac.uk).

In essence the literature offers lecturers perspectives on:

- the nature of academic identity and disciplinary content;
- student learning and development of learning competence;
- the personal relevance of study;
- the social impact of higher education.

The literature combines discussion of lecturers' perceptions of teaching and accounts of course design in a wide range of contexts with insights from qualitative research on student learning processes and outcomes. Readers who wish to explore in depth the ideas about learning, teaching, academic cultures and identities underlying the main features of the literature summarized above should consult the following texts: Perry, 1970; Stenhouse, 1975; Saljo, 1979; Rowntree, 1982; Chickering and Gamson, 1987; Brown and Atkins, 1988; Ramsden, 1992; Gibbs, 1992; Laurillard, 1993;

Steffe and Gale, 1995; Marton *et al.*, 1997; Nicol, 1997; Prosser and Trigwell, 1999; Dweck, 1999; Gent *et al.*, 1999; Henkel, 2000; Kogan, 2000; Becher and Trowler, 2001; Samuelowicz and Bain, 2001; Pang and Marton, 2003; Biggs, 2007; Land *et al.*, 2008.

I would not expect many lecturers to undertake this task as preparation for teaching practice, or even as part of a Postgraduate Certificate (PgCert) in Higher Education course. However, this brief list of the main writers may be a useful starting point for colleagues contemplating study at Masters level.

Constructive alignment: a unifying concept?

If one were to choose a particular text to start with, Biggs's (2007) account, which combines systematic course design and constructivist accounts of learning, is a helpful one. His account draws together most of the main strands in the literature and offers a practical language to discuss course design, teaching and assessment in relation to student learning. The following is a very brief summary of *constructive alignment*, but I think it is sufficient to provide a reasonably clear image of what a 'good' first year teacher might be doing in order to design learning activities which would address transition in the FYE. I will provide various practice examples of this in Chapters 3 and 4. In essence, Biggs defines a 'good' system of university teaching as one which aligns:

- stated learning objectives, expressed through verbs, which students are expected to enact;
- teaching methods and student activities chosen and implemented to exact relevant activity from students;
- assessment strategies which evaluate student accomplishment of stated objectives and motivate effort to improve.

Thus one can envisage a spectrum of learning levels in a course where students might achieve a low or middle ranking on assessment by demonstrating general coverage of topics, with some element of elaboration of the material. A higher level ranking would depend on the student developing capacity to enact processes described by terms like *hypothesize* or *apply* in new settings. Perhaps giving examples and showing a very thorough knowledge of relevant theory and methodology would also be highly valued. The likelihood of students obtaining higher rankings, and presumably deeper understanding, would be enhanced by teaching which focused on developing the key intellectual practices required.

I characterize such teaching as *student activity-centred*, implying a commitment, on the part of the lecturer, to a notion of teaching which values student learning over transmitting information and covering of content. How such commitment can be achieved and incentivized within the institution are topics I will discuss in Chapters 3, 4 and 5.

Some critiques of this literature

I divide this between critiques levelled by:

- disciplinary teachers;
- pedagogical specialists.

Disciplinary teachers

Academics often complain about the irrelevance of theoretical literature to their teaching practice. They may have a point and, if so, I believe they have an obligation to improve on the ideas they criticize. If colleagues accept that challenge, then we will all benefit from the reports of their findings. In the meantime, I believe there is a level of practitioner criticism which is as much a reflection of the low status accorded to teaching in their areas as it is to do with the demerits of the literature. Typical indicators are the statements that I have paraphrased here:

Referring to the literature

- 'It's all written by social scientists and has nothing to do with science/ engineering'
- 'The language is difficult and vague'
- 'We don't do the things they describe in my discipline'

Referring to the institutional context(s)

- 'We don't talk about teaching in my department, and if you do it's frowned upon'
- 'In our department, research is everything'
- 'In this university promotion is by research, not teaching'.

I can see some justification in these points, particularly as they illuminate the intersection of strategies for educational development through staff enrolment on Graduate Certificates and the institutional arrangements for incentivizing academic career pathways. For example, how many academics believe that effort expended on teaching and educational development, beyond compliance with probationary requirements, will make a positive contribution to their prospects of promotion and a professorship? Hence the often jaundiced views of academics who experience educational development through flawed institutional strategies for career and educational development. This is not to say that academics are a lost cause, indeed many do make use of educational development opportunities and bring about change in their teaching, albeit with concerns that this will not of itself help their career ambitions.

I believe the problem lies more with institutional systems and strategies than individual lecturers. The institutional forms of educational development – policy statements, general workshops and Graduate Certificates, for example – have had some success, particularly when conditioned by institutional interest in meeting external quality measures. More in-depth curriculum development projects are also successful, albeit mainly in the host sites. Consensus on what constitutes good or best practice remains elusive, however, and where benefits are seen in a particular course, institutions are not good at generalizing the beneficial measures to all courses. In effect, the results of such efforts have been patchy overall and it would be going too far to argue that a majority of academics engage in such activities beyond those which they must carry out as part of probationary arrangements.

The strategic approach to educational development lying behind these forms, whilst well intentioned, has been based largely on a progressive reform ethos, which prizes rationality, evidence and reference to academic literature. The Graduate Certificate courses of study for lecturers can be seen as a key means whereby institutions might enact this rationale, the idea being that the Certificate course approach, by encouraging lecturers to harness educational ideas from the literature to their practice, should set up the conditions for an enhanced student learning experience.

I believe that this reform strategy has relied too much on the goodwill and intrinsic motivation of individual lecturers and has not tackled serious disincentives such as institutionalized role conflict between teaching and research. Equally, there has been insufficient attention to reforming career structures, promotion criteria and reward mechanisms which would provide teaching careers on a par with the reward of research. Consequently lecturers can find themselves working in institutions which make great demands on them as teachers without necessarily providing the same clear rewards that they see applied to research.

My response to colleagues caught in this bind is twofold: First, it is not sufficient simply to attack the literature; you have to *read the literature into practice through decision making, choice of options, action research and reflection on teaching practice.* This is not easy, but hopefully the kind of activity I will describe at the end of this chapter offers some basic assistance, which can be amplified by the case studies in Chapters 3 and 4. Secondly, if you see the need to incentivize teaching as one condition of improving student learning, then actively lobby for a change in the incentive structure. The institutional constraints and barriers are likely to be tough, since they cannot usually be overcome by intellectual effort alone. This raises issues of institutional culture, strategy and management priorities, and I will take up these problems as matters of organizational development in Chapter 5.

Alternative pedagogical perspectives

In the meantime I would like to present some alternative views on the question of teaching students, from other pedagogical writers who do not fully embrace the tradition outlined above. My hope is that this may stimulate readers to review the current orthodoxy and develop a new agenda for educational development, which combines different perspectives.

Zukas and Malcolm (2007) have criticized the literature summarized above from a perspective rooted in adult education theory and practice and research in lifelong learning. They are coming from a tradition which encompasses informal learning, workplace learning and lifelong learning in communities. This tradition offers university teachers another way of thinking about students and learning processes, which can be linked to educational development in higher education. Their main points of dispute with the mainstream of the educational literature are that it:

- lacks development in relation to diversity and different student needs;
- presents learners as anonymous, mainly differentiated by mental models of learning approaches etc.;
- interprets pedagogy as sets of techniques applied by teachers to bring about certain responses in learners;
- incorporates significant environmental changes such as demands for employability/personal development planning as subordinate to the ruling paradigms of disciplinary teaching and not as opportunities to develop a new pedagogy of personalized learning;
- emphasizes the individual learner, and treats communal learning as a narrow technique-driven construct represented by the practicalities of 'group working';
- avoids questions of gender, ethnicity, selfhood etc.

By contrast, they propose a model of higher education emphasizing personal development as a key purpose, and defining development in terms of the growth of personhood, rather than the accumulation of employability skills and disciplinary knowledge. This is not some romantic denial of disciplinarity and skill development, but a challenge to go beyond their confines and embrace a wider notion of higher education's role in society.

Arguably they juxtapose two pedagogical approaches. One prizes teaching and learning in terms of the academic disciplines represented in university curricula and seeks a better understanding of relevant pedagogical theory and practice. The other advocates a less orthodox position, grounded in wider social and cultural perspectives on education. This alternative view is proposed as having potentially useful things to say about the ways in which university teaching can respond to the demands of wider access, diversity, employability and student personal development.

In essence I see Zukas and Malcolm raising a flag for the experience of learning characterized by individual ethical and existential growth, and channelled by a robust engagement with questions of power and equity in society and education. Diversity in class, gender, ethnicity, sexual orientation etc. are viewed not simply as 'pressures' arising from massification, to be managed and regulated in order to maintain system 'equilibrium'. Rather they are represented as the raw material of educational experience, to be debated and challenged in the course of study.

Whilst the critique may not do full justice to the writers cited above, its sharpness is a salutary reminder of the dangers of assuming that there is only one 'mainstream' of views which constitute the professional 'orthodoxy'. Their perspective should encourage further thinking about the purpose and practice of higher education, particularly in terms of:

- holistic interpretations of staff and student experiences of education;
- complex interpretations of diversity, employability, citizenship and lifelong learning.

Zukas and Malcolm provide a powerful comment on the socio-cultural context of higher education and how that might relate to the nature and development of pedagogy within institutions. I referred to this territory in Chapter 1 in terms of the potential for notions of lifelong learning to offer a vision of mass higher education which might be articulated through the curriculum in higher education. Zukas and Malcolm amplify my point, and extend it by setting out an account of the implications for pedagogy and educational development.

Key points from the literature

The constructivist approach to learning underpinning teaching, assessment and course design is arguably the dominant strand of thinking that is likely to be put before new lecturers. However, perspectives from adult education and specialists in lifelong learning pedagogy have useful points to contribute. These complementary strands of educational literature can be brought to bear on the FYE. The following distil the most important points of emphasis from both strands which might be used to develop curriculum:

Constructivist thinking:

- Importance of constructive alignment in designing first year classes
- Importance of student time spent on tasks designed to require active information processing to generate deeper understanding
- Importance of activities and processes entailing collaboration, self-regulation and metacognition

Adult lifelong learning:

- Importance of going beyond the boundaries of subject content and teaching practice to embrace diversity and the personal and social dimensions of learning
- Importance of avoiding narrow interpretations of education which privilege the interests of academic disciplines and/or employer-driven skills agendas

Neither strand is mutually exclusive; however, they need to be debated and applied to curriculum development in order to produce an expanded view of what university education is about. These points illuminate the discussion of teaching, learning and practical course design in Chapters 3 and 4.

What do we know about teaching first year students?

Whatever its merits, I think the literature described above is not sufficiently focused on the FYE. That being said, the quick answer to the question of 'what we know' about first year teaching and learning is, once again, 'quite a lot'. International work on the FYE has developed in parallel with massification and has gathered momentum in the last ten years. The trends in the FYE literature are complex, with the USA combining major scholarly work by individual academics with institutional initiatives by professional staff, at varying levels of scale. The National Resource Centre for the First Year Experience at the University of South Carolina is a useful starting point to explore American approaches (www.sc.edu/fye/center/contact.html).

In Australia the trend has been from small-scale localized initiatives, often driven by support staff, to more institutional strategizing involving academics in both teaching and senior management roles. The Australians have held annual Pacific Rim conferences on the First Year in Higher Education for a decade. Most of the past papers are available (www.fyhe.qut.edu.au/past_papers.html) and provide a valuable resource base of practical examples, theoretical discussion and institutional contacts.

Europe is catching up with the fourth European Conference on the First Year Experience held in 2009 (www.adm.heacademy.ac.uk/events/4th-european-first-year-experience-conference-2009). In the UK, both the Higher Education Academy and the Scottish QAA have sponsored research, publications, conferences and events on the FYE. The Scottish QAA has funded an ambitious project to develop a number of research reports on aspects of the FYE and these are listed in the Appendix (page 125).

Consequently, the FYE literature is very much open to discussion, debate and challenge against current experience. From that perspective I encourage readers to see themselves as potential producers of new literature, reflecting their experiences, rather than simply consumers of earlier ideas about the first year. Several recent reviews of the literature, including

Harvey *et al.* (2006) and Koch (2007), provide access to sources. The following literature summary distils the main trends in FYE over the last thirty years. This literature incorporates a range of concepts of the first year, which are now becoming more familiar in university discussions.

Main features of the literature

Some key points have emerged from the substantial international literature reporting research and practice, which help to define what might constitute a 'good' first year experience. The main points highlighted in the literature can be summarized as follows:

- nature and importance of FYE;
- curriculum imperatives;
- responses and measures to enhance first year;
- institutional priorities and enhancement;
- student surveys, assessment, evaluation and measurement of the student experience of first year.

Nature and importance of FYE

First year at university is seen as critical for students, academics and support specialists because it is during this period that new students have the experiences that form their initial understandings of academic and student life. If their understandings are accurate and realistic, and their experiences positive, then students are likely to progress and benefit from their time at university. However, if first year is a negative time then the likelihood of drop-out or underperformance is increased.

These are familiar generalizations but their significance for student well-being, institutional practice and social policy should not be underestimated. The personal and financial cost of making a weak adjustment to university can be considerable, and the aggregate costs of attrition to institutions and the public purse substantial. Consequently the FYE has become a focus for university-wide interest in co-ordinating initiatives to meet varied institutional missions including: improving retention rates; achieving positive quality audit returns; enhancing student academic success and general well-being.

This critical, formative period in an individual student's life is described in terms of challenge and change in academic, social and domestic/financial circumstances. Change involves issues of cultural adaptation and social integration as well as challenge to previous approaches to study, and is described as a period of *transition*. Specific academic difficulties encountered by students are identified, including:

- adapting to academic rigour;
- accepting academic writing conventions;
- standards of numeracy;
- time (on task) management;
- self-regulation of learning processes.

Difficulty is attributed to inadequate preparation for university, choosing the wrong course, mismatch in student/staff expectations, lack of support and the effectiveness of communication and feedback. The incidence of such difficulties is seen to have increased as student numbers have risen, to the extent that more systematic measures to support transition are required to avoid poor retention rates and to encourage student engagement and persistence.

In terms of the social composition of the student body, diversity in backgrounds, the needs of special populations and conflict between full-time study and part-time paid employment are increasingly regarded as significant features. Notions of student *assimilation, adjustment, engagement* and *empowerment* are proposed as constructs to explain transition and drive enhancement and evaluation of FYE. Social integration has been emphasized in the North American literature and has influenced thinking in the UK and Australia.

Curriculum imperatives

The first year curriculum can no longer be drawn simply in the form of broad, introductory classes aimed at providing foundational subject material to be built on in later years. Increasingly there is interest in engaging students in a more complex and challenging learning experience by treating the FYE as a foundation of learning activities entailing more inquiry-based formats and engendering employability and lifelong learning outcomes. In addition there is greater pressure to address gaps in expectations between lecturer and student perceptions of time commitment, for example. Also, disciplinary engagement and acceptable performance demand specific curriculum responses from first year onwards.

The trend is to advocate curriculum renewal to develop powerful learning environments with clear relevance to students' lives, rather than *ad hoc* and partial modifications of courses to meet perceived problems such as increased numbers, retention, skill gaps, lack of engagement etc. The imperative is to treat courses as social settings to engage collaborative learning, and overcome disengagement, by contrast to more traditional notions of 'content coverage'. Notions of 'employability' and 'work readiness' are discussed in terms of graduate attributes to be cultivated alongside academic disciplinary expertise and more traditional academic skills or literacies.

The specific emphasis in course design is increasingly targeted on assessment, for example making performance expectations clear from the outset, backed by early formative assessment, rather than relying on end of course 'marking/grading/ranking' methods. This model of curriculum development often fuels arguments within institutions for allocation of significant resources to first year, particularly in terms of the nature, training and quality of staff involved in teaching. This is an area ripe with research and development possibilities.

Responses and measures to enhance first year

The broad response has been to advocate a shift of emphasis from an assumption that in most cases students will survive and succeed, save for some students who will need special support, to an acceptance that first year is a key transitional stage in higher education which should be formally addressed for *all* entrants. In broad terms this may be expressed as a shift from a *deficit model*, where individual student inadequacies are in the foreground, to a *developmental model*, which views the FYE as a system of interrelated dimensions, including course design and pedagogical activity, which impacts all students in the year group. A broad trend is also manifest in the pendulum swing over time from a very student-supportive emphasis, often with a strong counselling ethos, to a greater emphasis on introducing students to academic rigour, indeed demanding this of them.

I am inclined towards the developmental model; however, that is not to say that individuals will not need particular attention and specific support measures to acknowledge special needs and respond to crises. It is more a matter of questioning assumptions and revising their efficacy in the face of the changed circumstances of a mass higher education system.

Responsibility for providing academic support has tended to fall on the shoulders of academics with a particular commitment to the FYE, and may be characterized in terms of a combination of academic administration and pastoral care. Staff involved can include lecturers in the roles of first year class co-ordinators, personal tutors, members of staff/student committees and, to an extent, Deans and Vice Deans. Staple activities include selection and ongoing advice on course choice and change options, which are seen as essential to allow early transfers when initial course choices prove to be inappropriate. 'At risk' monitoring and progress checking is also under-taken at course level and should be followed up by personal tutoring and mentoring. Individual lecturers and tutors also play their part through their daily teaching practice and assessment, although this may not be accorded as much value and reward as FYE specialists would wish for.

Measures

Central support services have historically tended to bear the brunt of provision that might be commonly understood to be targeted at the FYE, particularly in terms of orientation events, study skill support and subsequent support for individuals in financial or personal difficulty. This has given rise to a pattern of systematic FYE activities, which has become familiar, and includes measures such as: pre-entry information events; summer schools; freshers' week orientation events and induction programmes.

The aim of these measures is to:

- demystify the transition to university;
- introduce staff/student roles, rights, responsibilities;
- illuminate expectations and describe appropriate study practices.

In practice they tend to emphasize providing information about support services and attempts to familiarize students with academic rigour. This latter objective may take the form of workshops with associated resources focused on:

- academic writing;
- time management;
- exam preparation;
- use of online resources;
- library services; and
- the nature of critical thinking and differences from school/college.

The main thrust has focused on improving skills, by 'bringing them up' to the levels required for university. However, there is also a growing interest in developing *academic literacies*, where the emphasis is on issues such as the enculturations entailed in coming to university and also the nature of academic writing, for example Barton, 1994; Lea and Street, 1997, 1998; Lillis, 2001; Lillis and Turner, 2001; Lea, 2004; Heikkila and Lonka, 2006.

These measures can be integrated to form transition support programmes spread over the first year, operated at university, faculty and department levels. For example:

- Freshers' week orientation events and information dissemination
- Class induction programmes to introduce staff/student roles, rights and responsibilities and familiarize students with academic rigour e.g. exam preparation, nature of critical thinking and differences from upper school/college
- Stand-alone skill-building programmes, particularly ICT, academic writing, numeracy
- Ongoing advice by academics on course choice and change options
- Course-level 'at risk' monitoring systems

- Personal tutoring and mentoring provided by academics/peers
- Peer Assisted Study Support (PASS) activities and Supplemental Instruction (SI) programmes, often targeted at particular classes/subject matter that regularly prove troublesome to students
- Remedial tuition (maths is a particular focus)

Features of this listing of activities will be familiar as aspects of the services provided by central support departments, endorsed by academic staff and prized by institutions as part of their marketing and quality management efforts. However, they may not fall under any strategic authority for central direction, being more or less devolved to particular departments and often championed by individuals. Also, student engagement with what is on offer may be more or less voluntary until some crisis forces engagement. Crucially, such programmes tend to stand alongside mainstream teaching and assessment activities and lack the impact of integrated activities. The implications of this semi-detached approach are discussed in Chapter 3.

In terms of pedagogical responses and measures beyond those outlined above, there is growing support for more active teaching methods and increased student collaboration within courses, and the development of learning communities is advocated. There is also increasing interest in 'whole course' redesign using the idea of 'constructive alignment' (Biggs, 2007) and incorporating many of the foregoing measures in the course designs. Typically these measures are underpinned by the constructivist principles of student learning outlined above. Constraints on these trends include: limited resources, pressure on academics to prioritize research and underdeveloped institutional strategic support. The idea of 'transition pedagogy' (Kift, 2004, 2005, 2008) is a major challenge to these constraints.

Institutional priorities and enhancement

Institutions in a mass system have difficult strategic directions to navigate. Do they stick with traditional academic concerns about rigour and standards, linked to managerial concerns with retention and quality audit? Or do they move beyond those perspectives and re-engineer their activities to reflect a world where there are not only more students but different kinds of students, and more acute pressures from potential employers to develop graduate attributes related to employability? Is it possible to steer a middle course and address all of the issues?

There has been a tendency for institutions to emphasize retention and progression rates as strategic issues, often focused by concerns regarding wider access and diversity. Concerns to achieve good external quality ratings and a healthy response in the National Student Survey (NSS) accentuate institutional desire to enhance the student experience, with the FYE as a major focal point. The state and public opinion have played a part in pressing these issues with institutional leaders, with various annual league tables exerting considerable pressure on institutions to 'deal with' any perceived weaknesses which might result in a loss of league ranking. Whilst such pressures for transparent performance data are inevitable when large sums of taxpayers' money are spent on higher education, I am concerned that responses in the form of narrowly focused thinking, driven by short-term objectives, will distort and hold back more holistic enhancement of the FYE.

In keeping with this concern, there is a now strong trend amongst FYE specialists to advocate holistic enhancement of the student experience as the basis for strategic development, as opposed to reliance on fragmented initiatives aimed at specific problem issues. As institutional policy makers take greater interest in the FYE, specialists can grasp significant opportunities to extend their arguments for enhancement of the FYE. When institutions take a strategic interest in the FYE, to improve retention for example, they may be persuaded to conduct institutional research on the student experience and to develop policy and strategic action plans that address a full range of academic and support activities, including curriculum and staff development. With implementation of such plans comes reporting through academic committees dealing with academic policy, student experience, quality assurance and the like, with consequent opportunities to revise assumptions, change structures and enhance practice.

At that stage of institutional development, the nature and extent of academic staff commitment is thrown into the foreground, and combined with the central support service contribution for review aimed at developing greater efficiency and effectiveness. In practice this can focus on joining up measures to improve pre-entry decision making and preparedness for study, followed by systematic, year-long induction post-entry, with accompanying changes in support systems, course design and pedagogy. Advocacy for strong links between academic and student support processes usually accompanies this tendency. There is also scope to develop substantial projects to improve teaching and assessment by redesigning courses and making best use of technology.

Key sources: supporting students and improving teaching

For readers who want to go beyond my summary, the following authors provide a substantial account of influential work: Tinto, 1975; Barr and Lee Upcraft, 1990; Gabelnick *et al.*, 1990; Kuh *et al.*, 1991, 2005, 2008; Pascarella and Terenzini, 1991, 2005; Astin, 1993; Tinto, 1993; Tinto *et al.*, 1994; McInnis *et al.*, 1995; Blimling and Whitt, 1999; Braxton, 2000; Cook, 2003; Kuh, 2003; Lowe and Cook, 2003; Braxton *et al.*, 2004; Kift, 2004, 2005; Yorke and Longden, 2004, 2007, 2008; Kift and Nelson, 2005; Krause, 2005; Krause *et al.*, 2005; Manning *et al.*, 2006; Seidman, 2006; Porter and Swing,

2006; Zepke *et al.*, 2006; Wingate, 2007; Cook and Rushton, 2008; Krause and Coates, 2008; Lewis and Castley, 2008.

As with the general literature on teaching, I would not expect lecturers to read all of this material before teaching first year classes, or writing assignments for PgCerts etc. This is more the basis of masters-level reading.

Student surveys, assessment, evaluation and measurement of the student experience of first year

Allied to the work reported above, there has been a growing interest in gathering data and information about higher education and its impact on students, in order to manage provision better and improve quality. For example, the series of surveys carried out in Australia over the last twenty years (Krause *et al.*, 2005) has been influential on FYE activity. At time of writing this survey is due to be repeated in 2009/10.

At international level the Organization for Economic Co-operation and Development (OECD, 2008) has underlined the importance of this data-gathering activity, and a number of national strategies are in place to estimate student satisfaction and engagement.

A number of valuable surveys have been undertaken around the world and arguably have had some effect in assisting higher education institutions (HEIs) and other stakeholders in their efforts to enhance the quality of the student experience. The main purposes for national surveys have been to:

- influence teachers and teaching;
- improve the quality of educational provision and student support.

This brief account is provided to assist readers in quickly accessing information about other surveys, which may be helpful in considering their approach and findings. Three national surveys are noted here.

United Kingdom

- National Student Survey – NSS: www.heacademy.ac.uk/assets/York/documents/ourwork/research/NSS_2008_questionnaire_online_version.pdf.
  The NSS comprises eight dimensions/scales of satisfaction plus a choice of additional dimensions which HEIs can incorporate to meet local issues. It has been conducted annually since 2005, with some Scottish HEIs participating since 2007. The theoretical base is the same as the Australian CEQ, emphasizing the importance of students' perceptions of their learning context and the impact this has on their learning outcomes.

Australia

- Australasian Survey of Student Engagement – AUSSE: www.acer.edu.au/ ausse/.
  The AUSSE builds on the US National Survey of Student Engagement.
- In addition to AUSSE, a new survey is being developed by the Australian Council for Education Research (ACER) to extend the range of information on the quality of the student experience: uniTEST (unitest.acer.edu.au/).
  This is being developed to assist selection and recruitment by assessing thinking skills associated with successful university study.

United States of America

- National Survey of Student Engagement – NSSE: nsse.iub.edu/pdf/ NSSE2008_US_English_Paper.pdf.
  The NSSE comprises 42 items in five groups for 'comparative bench-marking' based on Chickering and Gamson's (1987) seven principles for good practice in undergraduate education, and other related works. It has been ongoing since 2001 and is linked to the Defining Effective Educational Practice research project (DEEP: www.nsse.iub.edu/ institute/index.cfm?view=deep/index). The NSSE is designed to investi-gate student engagement, and the data are used systematically to identify HEIs which perform above their benchmark for engagement, and then to investigate what influential factors and practices are involved.

All of these surveys show that the territories designated as 'student experience' and 'educational quality' are being differentiated and sub-jected to scrutiny through different survey methods. The connections between these efforts to gather useful information about the experience and impact of higher education, and the efforts of FYE specialists to improve the first year, have still to be fully described. However, there is a clear need to balance quantitative and qualitative information about the nature and quality of student experience in deciding the most appropri-ate ways for institutions to enhance and improve provision. In meeting these needs several key constructs have been advanced to offer a vision of what the FYE might seek to achieve, and what form of first year is most appropriate to that vision.

Engagement and empowerment: two key concepts for the FYE

I should like to turn now from the literature of the FYE to discuss two terms that are becoming common in pedagogical discussion. This adds to the account of FYE terminology, such as *transition*, in Chapter 1.

Engagement is one of those terms in HE discourse that has become part of the professional vocabulary. This may result in devaluation of meaning, and perhaps some cynicism from academics who think of it as just more 'jargon' from education bureaucrats. However, I believe that, if it is used with common sense, it can progress activity by fine-tuning discussion and decision making. It also has descriptive power to illuminate terms like 'active learning'. The following list of meanings that might be associated with engagement are offered to stimulate reflection:

- attending;
- settling in;
- participating;
- seeking clarification;
- reflecting.

Empowerment is perhaps less commonly used, but I have observed it being deployed in discussions of study skills, for example where being empowered is related to the power over learning which students can achieve by developing study skills. However, I believe that it can also be understood in a more holistic way, concerned with staff/student collaboration about the nature and practice of teaching and assessment. Here are some further possible interpretations of student empowerment, to stimulate reflection:

- developing self-confidence and self-efficacy;
- achieving accomplished performance;
- self-regulation of study;
- contributing to evaluation and development of course designs.

Student views of engagement and empowerment

My own research (Johnston and Kochanowska, 2009) using focus groups with students from a range of Scottish HEIs is illuminating, as we simply asked the participants to respond to the terms, and did not give any hint of our own views. Here are some student statements to give a flavour of how students themselves respond to these terms.

Engagement/disengagement

- Lecturers having no enthusiasm = students having no enthusiasm
- Poor lecturers (just reading from the slides), lecturers not turning up or not making an effort is disengaging
- Lack of communication – where, who, what etc. is disengaging
- Don't blame lecturers for not helping students that are not engaged
- Need to get away from the passive learning; moving from more passive learning (spoon feeding) to more active engagement

- Relying on computers, not people, is disengaging
- First year doesn't count, so students will not take it very seriously – just have to pass
- The presence of students at uni who are not sure why they are there is disengaging
- Having to take five disparate unlinked subjects in first year/being forced to do subjects you don't want to do is disengaging. You only do enough for a bare pass in the subjects you don't want to do

Empowerment/disempowerment

- Broadening learning (learning how to use journals etc., reading around subject, not getting stuck on working to exam) is empowering
- Being involved in decision making – e.g. more practical work
- Turning up and just taking notes is disempowering – need to be involved
- Realizing you have more potential to change the way things are done
- Deadlines all coming together is disempowering
- As numbers increase, empowerment and engagement decrease
- Not getting feedback from an assessment before the next one is due is disempowering
- Not knowing how you are performing/whether what you are doing is worth a pass/fail is disempowering

A useful exercise would be to compare the foregoing statements with your views of how you think your students might perceive their first year experiences. Equally, gathering views from your own students would illuminate 'jargon' terms like engagement and empowerment, and give them tangible meaning in the context you share with your students. A procedure to carry out such an exercise is described in Chapter 3.

Pedagogical connections: the literatures combined

The foregoing discussion of FYE complements the emphasis in the broader literature on learning processes outlined at the beginning of this chapter. In that general literature, students are portrayed as learning by constructing meanings, and developing reflection and academic self-regulation. These attributes might be adopted as key learning outcomes from first year onwards and embedded in course designs for teaching, feedback and assessment practice. This approach can be linked with an emphasis on personal development and self-efficacy as key graduate attributes, which may serve the requirements of potential employers but which have added value as tools for effective citizenship and lifelong learning.

Good teaching tends to be described these days in terms of devising tasks and activities that bring about learning, where learning is characterized as constructive, collaborative and in some sense 'deep' or 'applied'. Classroom activities such as electronic voting systems, one-minute-paper techniques etc. are gaining ground as partial measures to overcome the passivity of traditional lectures and engage students more effectively in understanding concepts. Social and academic integration via collaborative learning in groups and teams is an increasingly common feature. There is increased interest in assessment and feedback generally, and peer and self-assessment in particular, as essential to building academic engagement and empowerment from first year onwards. The FYE-specific material is becoming suffused with the social constructivist ethos and discourse.

Defining a 'good' FYE

Taken together, these ideas from the literature suggest a multi-level approach to first year, involving institutional leaders and academics as well as service professionals, with a significant uplift in the status of first year in institutional decision making and resource allocation. In effect a step change is being advocated in the attention paid to the first year at all levels within institutions. Based on the literature, a professional definition of a 'good' FYE can be cast in terms of:

- student participation in powerful learning environments founded on the constructivist approach to learning;
- staff, students and institutions collaborating to create supportive learning communities;
- staff developing 'whole year' responses to transition, engagement and empowerment, which form coherent foundations for degree programmes;
- emphasis on explicit measures to encourage confidence building and self-efficacy, rather than assuming students will simply 'mature' over time;
- legitimizing difficulties as material for reflection and change rather than evidence of failure;
- building a community of support amongst the students and staff;
- accepting that diversity is a source of varied experiences and backgrounds which can be drawn on to enhance engagement with learning and as a focus for empowerment;
- expanding the horizons of the curriculum to develop a higher education experience that involves students with a range of social, cultural and economic issues, which might combine to develop their sense of citizenship.

When joined together, the literatures offer an increased understanding of how students learn, an expanded array of pedagogies to enhance learning and a detailed account of the FYE as a site where these ideas might be deployed to support student transition and engagement.

Questions, concepts and practicalities arising from the literature

I have described teaching as a process of decision making, and I now suggest five focal questions about teaching that need to be considered by lecturers and addressed by pedagogical literature. The following table poses the five questions and selects some concise headline responses distilled from the literature.

Table 2.1 Teaching decisions: five focal questions

Focal questions	Selected responses
1 **Learning process**: what actions and experiences constitute the development of student understanding and progression?	Collaborative, cumulative and constructive
2 **Learners**: what characteristics describe the ideal student place in the learning process?	Engaged and empowered
3 **Nature of thinking**: what is the extent of awareness and responsiveness to knowledge?	Rich structures of awareness – deep, reflective, analytical, creative
4 **Design for learning**: what is the plan for teaching the course (content, methods, assessment etc.)	Constructively aligned
5 **Applications of learning**: what kinds of use will students make of knowledge?	Practical, analytical and creative

How would we start to translate these higher order concepts into classroom realities?

What to do about pedagogical knowledge – a practical approach

At the beginning of this chapter I suggested that pedagogical knowledge should be used, and that a practical exercise would be provided in putting that knowledge to use. The approach described here was developed within an HEA-accredited course on teaching and learning in higher education, aimed at probationary lecturers. It is based on the premise that two or more lecturers working as a peer critiquing group can make significant gains in practical understanding of the extent to which ideas about teaching can illuminate actual teaching sessions, in their local context.

It is time-efficient, and has proved a useful and stimulating activity for several hundred probationary lecturers across a full range of disciplinary fields, with the exception of medicine. Peer groups can be created by bringing together departmental colleagues, or colleagues in other areas. There can be benefit in working with somebody from outside your own discipline, in that assumptions have to be challenged, and there is also the opportunity to observe and discuss different approaches in the light of a common idea about teaching. Whilst the approach seems most appropriate for new lecturers, it has been used to good effect by colleagues with twenty-five years' experience, giving them a valuable opportunity to debate and reflect on their engrained teaching practices, through discussion and reading.

The basic procedure, once a peer group has been formed, is to meet and discuss some of the ideas from the literature that seem relevant to one's own teaching and seem to show promise as a guide to enhanced practice. Colleagues can elect to read a common text, perhaps a chapter on teaching large first year classes, or a paper on the relationship between lecturers' concepts of teaching and their practice. A useful starting position is to take the broad idea from the literature of getting students more actively engaged and link it to situations in your own teaching where students are clearly not as active as you would want. The examples in Table 2.2 illustrate several possible starting positions.

Table 2.2   Student engagement: issues and strategy

Focal issue	Practical strategy
Reversing a decline in student attendance at lectures	Implementing greater student activity during lectures e.g. quizzes, buzz groups
Encouraging more student contributions in tutorials	Avoiding going into mini-lecture mode e.g. planning discussion tasks for students to carry out in sub-groups; practise your facilitation skills

The peer work can be spread over several stages and over the duration of a course. As a rule of thumb, the aim is to arrange up to three sequenced observations of teaching and three related critiquing sessions in a given semester/year. If possible, plan critiquing meetings to take place towards the beginning, the middle and the end of the semester/year, to give a sense of progression and to explore the impact of any interventions on student responses and performance.

Each of the critiquing exercises must include an observation of a colleague's teaching, preceded by a discussion of the theoretical issues involved, followed by a critiquing meeting, to unpack the session. The inclusion of critical discussion of ideas about teaching is essential as a means of ensuring that theory and practice are integrated. It is not enough simply to comment on the actions observed without reference to what the colleague was trying to achieve. Each member of the peer group undertakes to engage in and document each of the three peer critiquing exercises. This gives every member direct experience of:

- formulating a theoretically informed strategy drawing on the literature;
- observing/being observed putting the strategy into practice;
- giving/receiving feedback on practice in relation to theory.

The critiquing exercises should include:

- a preliminary discussion to establish each person's focal issue(s), his or her proposed strategy and the theoretical reasoning behind the strategy;
- an observation of your peer's teaching – which may take any of the usual forms, e.g. lectures, tutorials, workshops, or may focus on a new setting;
- a post-observation critiquing meeting to discuss: what happened during the teaching and how effective it seemed to be; an identification of alternative practices and their relative merits; planning future practice. Observers should press for theoretically informed justifications of actions and future plans;
- a review of actions your colleague has taken on points discussed at the previous critiquing session and his or her plans for further action.

The amount of time involved is clearly something to be negotiated, and timing will depend on participants' opportunities to try out their plans. However, if this exercise is implemented in full it should assist in developing a theoretically informed experience of key elements in university teaching – planning, implementing and evaluating practice.

For a probationer, this approach should assist in developing more skilful teaching practice and a more confident appreciation of what educational literature can, and cannot, contribute to the teaching role. In addition, this exercise should provide probationers with valuable evidence of a thoughtful and practical approach to teaching, which can be deployed in annual progress reviews and the final confirmation review. More experienced lecturers may find this approach useful as part of their approach to introducing change in their teaching practice, or simply to check out the continued efficacy of methods which inevitably become routine.

3

The first year experience and the academic mainstream

Introduction

Chapter 1 looked briefly into the daily lives of lecturers and identified some difficult teaching challenges they can face with first year classes. Key influences on those teaching challenges include:

- national policies to widen access and increase the relevance of degrees to the economy;
- increased state intervention in the sector to ensure educational quality;
- student financial pressures and part-time employment;
- different stakeholder perceptions in universities.

These influences interact in shaping the student learning environment at all points and key features include:

- changing traditional teaching methods developed for an elite system, to meet the needs of mass enrolments;
- demand for a wider range of graduate attributes with perhaps greater emphasis on 'critical thinking' type attributes;
- need to negotiate student involvement with study on grounds of interest and relevance, given the pressures of paid work on their time.

However, the basic equation which lecturers face in many first year classes must often look something like this:

Massification = mass enrolments = large classes = more assessments = more work

In Chapter 2 I described some of the insights into student learning and teaching practice from the professional literature, which might be used to help lecturers meet these challenges. I also suggested a practical teaching exercise, involving peer observation and discussion of practice, to help take the theories out of the library and into the classroom, in effect concentrating on the pedagogical response to massification of higher education.

This chapter will develop these themes, by exploring ways in which a lecturer's commitment to the FYE can be incorporated into the mainstream of academic activity. The chapter is organized around two interlinked aspects:

- Academic mainstreaming of FYE: student engagement, lecturer/student perceptions; teaching and learning; assessment; study skills and information literacy; building a teaching profile; educational development
- Central service model: current perspectives; partnerships for mainstreaming

Engaging students in the curriculum

The task is to identify modes of organizing and conducting first year teaching that are more likely to engage more students and lead them to confident learning practice. Allied to this is the need for institutions to review their commitment to students in first year by directing institutional resources into educational development aimed at enhancing student transition, engagement and empowerment. Without such resource commitment, it is difficult to be confident that staff commitment *alone* will achieve significant enhancement of the FYE. Consequently I believe we need an institutional process of educational development at both policy committee and department levels that matches individual commitment with appropriate resources and incentives to encourage and reward individuals.

I have labelled the process involved 'mainstreaming'. This is to indicate that the educational change involved need not be viewed as an extreme shift in practice, but more as an accentuation of features already present in first year courses. There will inevitably be variation in the forms and extent to which such features are present across institutions. Nonetheless, there should be a basis in current reality which can be developed. The emphasis is on what lecturers need to do, but I will also advance some suggestions concerning central services and consider issues such as study skills.

Mainstreaming the first year experience and scaffolding transition

A key FYE strategy is for academics to move transition issues into the mainstream of their courses, through enhancements of course design, teaching, assessment and progress monitoring. The aim is to create a learning experience that helps students work to their full potential and offers additional support to those who continue to struggle. This approach requires moving, both conceptually and in practice, beyond the common legacy of over-reliance on early orientation and introduction strategies as the main response to transition and overemphasis on retention as the major first year issue. The desired position is one where existing first year courses are specifically designed to support students making a transition to higher education and build a foundation for academic success. As a rule of thumb, it is sensible to assume that students are in transition until they have completed at least the first year of their course.

The academic mainstreaming approach argues for greater academic staff involvement to treat the FYE as a year-long initiative. Staff can do this via explicit measures to encourage student academic and social engagement during transition. This extends the discussion of transition, engagement and empowerment by describing the lecturer's role in making these experiences more transparent in relation to teaching, learning and assessment. The mainstreaming approach also advocates greater partnership between academics and specialist central services, going beyond student referrals, for example, to incorporation of some service values and skills in teaching practice. In addition there is a need to revisit earlier notions of 'study skills' to adopt more sophisticated models geared to the realities of the 'net generation'.

Finally, I suggest there is an urgent need to introduce much more systematic 'institutional research' to illuminate the particular local characteristics and circumstances relating to the FYE. An example might be statistical analysis of institutional data sets, to generate information about student experience and performance in general (Yorke and Longden, 2004) and to illuminate the local understanding of key concepts such as 'academic failure' (Wimshurst and Allard, 2008). The outcomes of such research can help clarify conceptions and target actions to areas where they will do most good.

Key characteristics of mainstreaming

The aim is to have students spending more time on challenging academic and skill building tasks and less time on didactic teaching. As far as possible student support should come through the curriculum, and macro issues like diversity and employability should be explicit features. Good quality feedback on performance leading to improvement in performance, further reflection and superior self-regulation is an essential feature. The following matrix (Table 3.1) summarizes some key components of mainstreaming.

Table 3.1   Mainstreaming: key features and actions

What is involved?	How is it to be achieved?
Shifting staff perceptions of the FYE from a 'retention' focus to an emphasis on 'student success'	Collectively agree an image of success and commit to promoting it. Set high expectations for students. Monitor underperformance and intervene quickly. Headline some 'big' concepts of HE e.g. a preparation for lifelong learning; employability, citizenship

Developing first year classes within an explicit framework of early transition stages	Scaffold student transition experiences in stages at pre-entry, freshers' week, and first 4–6 weeks, through a coherent sequence of interconnected communications, activities and monitoring of engagement
Dedicating teaching staff time to FYE and where possible dedicate physical and virtual space to first year students	Deploy lecturers with explicit remits to develop first year classes, to address transition. Give them resources and responsibility to deliver. Boost the status of first year teaching. Focus on closing gaps between lecturer's assumptions about prerequisite knowledge, skills and motivations and the actual positions of students. Prioritize creating a feedback and assessment strategy which offers varied methods, timely feedback and progression. Monitor student engagement in terms of attendance, participation and performance to identify points for intervention
Embedding activities throughout first year classes to address transition, engagement and empowerment	Make teaching and assessment strategy transparent to students, and identify expectations. Design and introduce activities where students have to collaborate with others, evaluate their own performance and take responsibility for changes. Target activities on complex academic skills as well as subject content e.g. academic writing, information literacy. Develop explicit skill development criteria in subject assignments; acknowledge the skill components in assignments and give them significant weight in marking. Introduce systematic feedback aimed at improving performance and developing self-regulation

This practical guide provides a basic template and checklist for mainstreaming, which can simplify and speed up the process of development. It can be used by an individual lecturer to mainstream FYE and transition issues in his or her classes; however, I recommend that where possible there is a departmental commitment, in order to maximize impact and ensure greater consistency.

Lecturer concerns: teaching and the student experience

Since most of the activities discussed in this chapter will be carried out by lecturers and will not get very far without their commitment, it makes sense to start from their perceptions. The following statements come from new lecturers attending a three-day introductory course which provides an overview of teaching and learning issues in contemporary higher education. The course is jointly run by two UK universities; one is a chartered institution with a strong commitment to research and the other fits more closely the profile of a post-1992 'wider access' institution. The participants are drawn from a variety of disciplines and backgrounds. There is usually a varied profile of prior teaching experience including Graduate Teaching Assistant work and organizational training activities, but the majority are quite inexperienced.

As part of the course the whole group is given an interactive lecture on the implications of theories of student learning for teaching in mass higher education. The content of that lecture includes a number of the main features of the literature described in Chapter 2, including an introduction to constructive alignment. There is also a brief introductory presentation of points describing the FYE as:

- a theme for enhancing learning;
- a strategic response to massification and diversity;
- a context for student engagement and successful learning;
- a focus on transition, progress, retention and success.

The statements reproduced below arise from interactive exercises during the lecture. They are presented so that readers can compare them with their own views. The participants are asked to identify some of their personal concerns about their teaching role, and these points are a representative selection:

- meeting institutional requirements;
- confidence;
- getting students engaged;
- coping with large numbers and diversity;
- encouraging 'deep' approaches in learning.

The participants were also asked to identify what they saw as important parts of the first year that they thought their students needed to experience. Answers included:

- enjoyment and belonging;
- recogniszing opportunities and being self-regulated;
- knowing what's expected;
- interest and motivation;
- a good transition;
- support.

This is a varied list of potential areas where the lecturer is likely to feel both responsible and to some extent vulnerable. Practical strategies, supportive colleagues and systematic educational development are therefore highly desirable. None of these items is susceptible to 'easy answers' and all require a professional process entailing pedagogical thinking, skilled practice and reflection. The approaches outlined in this chapter are intended to illustrate this process and share some examples of that process being carried through in different contexts.

Student expectations

The student experience of learning in first year can be observed very early on, in familiar and quizzical expressions of concern, often tied to assessment, such as:

- 'I'm not really sure what they (lecturers) expect in an essay'
- 'I suppose there is no right or wrong answer here; as long as you argue your point well then you'll pass'
- 'I guess three sides in the exam book will be enough'

All three points seem to fit well with the statements lecturers made above of their perception of what students needed to get out of their FYE – knowing what's expected in particular. That being said, a busy lecturer's first response to the student sense of vagueness about expectations can be a sense of frustration that students:

- 'Don't seem to know the difference between description and analysis'
- 'Can't supply evidence to back up opinions'
- 'Expect to be spoon fed all the time'

No doubt lecturers, student counsellors and students themselves will readily appreciate these paraphrases and supply others of their own. These snapshots of student need are valuable indicators of basic issues where early effort might be best expended. The task, of course, is finding efficient and effective ways of meeting student needs for clarity, which benefit most students and and can be implemented by lecturers with relative ease.

Developing mainstreaming: strategy, stages and measures

In combination, these various reported statements illustrate an awareness that teaching is not simply a matter of transmitting content to rooms full of more or less acquiescent students, but a more complex and demanding educational enterprise. In effect the common sense of lecturers and students mirrors the modern view of university teaching as a professional activity related to scholarship and pedagogical research. One fundamental item from the list of points generated by the lecturers on my three-day course should serve to exemplify the pedagogical challenges (Table 3.2).

Table 3.2   Pedagogical challenges and lecturer perceptions

Lecturer concerns about teaching	Lecturer perceptions of important student experiences
Getting students engaged	Knowing what's expected

If one were to help students to know what is expected of them early on in the semester, that action could be expected to help them settle in and begin to engage actively with topics and coursework. Strategic learning objectives for this phase might include reducing anxiety and countering tendencies to disorganized study, whilst encouraging a more confident and targeted approach to learning tasks. The core of the work would be a sequence of focal issues, presented proactively as an essential part of the course. This might include challenging the idea that pre-university study methods are all that is required and that study 'help' is really only for weaker students. The staff attitude needs to be very positive and the activities very practical to capture attention and commitment. Contributions from more experienced students who can attest the benefits of active engagement will help, as will clear connections to improved assessment marks.

If embedded help is spread progressively over the first semester it will be a robust way of getting students more engaged with their subjects and more appreciative of what university study entails. A good first semester is a major stepping stone to a good first year transition. In second semester the transition plan can be a combination of reinforcement of first semester topics, introduction of new or more complex topics and increased expectations for more independent and self-regulated learning. There will also be a need to give some students more individual support and perhaps enlist support from specialist services.

The measures chosen should be a combination of well-designed information resources, perhaps in a handbook format, complemented by time spent in lectures explaining the expectations and giving students some relevant exercises. Traditional 'study skill' areas such as time management strategies and academic writing can form the basis of activity but they must be clearly linked to the kinds and levels of performance expected in the class and in coursework. Examples of good, bad and indifferent work can be explained and made available for reference.

A strategic response to the challenges in this example is to think of the interventions as a sequence of related and enabling 'stages' of transition, where lecturer action can influence student experience. In practice, each transition stage is being addressed by specific measures embedded in the overall course design plan for contact time, online resources, assessment and feedback – just like subject content decisions, in fact. It would be practical to devise a separate plan to address transition issues, simply to ensure that they receive equal attention with subject content decisions. However, I must stress that the actual operationalization of such a plan should be an integral part of the course, and not delivered as a parallel or purely online unit, given the risk of decontextualization and reduced impact.

Teaching, learning and assessment: pedagogical transparency

The basic perspective is to motivate more students to become more engaged by giving them very clear messages about what is expected and, crucially, giving them practical activities to develop relevant performance. It is no longer sufficient simply to teach and examine; we must develop greater capacity to give constructive feedback and encourage students to regulate their learning more effectively. As first year cohorts become larger and more diverse this task must attract greater priority, in order to maintain standards, keep up pass rates and motivate students to persist and excel. These priorities will be more acute in circumstances where institutions, or particular courses, face competitive recruitment and perhaps cannot afford to turn away students whose entry level qualifications may be judged weak.

My key principle is to make the first year learning environment as transparent, welcoming and engaging as possible. Implementing this notion of pedagogical transparency at its broadest level involves:

- explaining what is required for success, what students need to do, how lecturers are going to help them and how students can learn to help themselves and each other;
- humanizing teaching by organizing class contact time to involve regular student discussion and contributions;
- offering some degree of personalization of courses, perhaps by online systems;
- providing a consistent level of current information, backed by usable web-based resources and accessible staff;

- exposing students to a variety of teaching, learning and assessment methods;
- creating clear assessment criteria, using marking schemes consistently and providing models and exemplars of good student work;
- encouraging students to ask for help, and also to develop skills and persistence.

Teaching: implementing pedagogical transparency

There is no substitute for making informed changes in your own teaching practice, but it can help to have an approach and some examples as a guide. The following approach combines my own experiences with material distilled from the practical literature. New teachers may find this material useful in clarifying what they might do, whilst more experienced teachers may find that they have already tried some of the approaches and will have their own examples to compare and contrast.

In terms of pedagogy, the shift in emphasis is from students 'being taught' to 'experiencing learning'. This shift implies encouraging student self-regulation of their learning processes and reflection/self-assessment, combined with effective peer/tutor feedback. I have expressed the approach somewhat more bluntly as the 'what' and the 'how' of developing courses where this pedagogical approach is explicit (Table 3.3).

Table 3.3 Pedagogical transparency in action

What to do	How to do it
Unpack the 'success skills' for the discipline and your course design. Relate them to criteria for excellent performance. Clarify likely student expectations/engagement in terms of previous learning and the realities of university study and assessment	List obvious study skills for your discipline. Add graduate attributes for employability and a linked academic characteristic e.g. inquiring mind, critical analysis. Express the items as learning objectives/assessment criteria for the foundational level of study
Repackage these skills as part of teaching/assessment practice, and give class time to helping students develop success skills and strategies	Create micro teaching activities to raise awareness and build skills. Schedule these in class time for points of maximum relevance e.g. exam preparation sessions immediately prior to exams. As far as possible deploy the activities in small group sessions to allow discussion. Make activities available online for self-managed reinforcement. Emphasize the expectation of developing greater independence and academic judgement

Target critical times for disengagement/disorganization. Take account of any diversity issues e.g. different backgrounds, special needs	Identify assignment deadlines and concentrate relevant skill building sessions accordingly. Reinforce messages about seeking help if contemplating drop-out. Monitor attendance, late submission and poor results patterns and seek out the students who seem to be disengaging
Revise assessment criteria and marking schemes. Identify troublesome disciplinary topics or procedures which tend to depress student success. Devise 'success' sessions to address the criteria and the troublesome areas	Use varied assessments and don't over-rely on 'tick box' or short answer formats. Run tutorials as 'nuts and bolts' sessions, where students 'unpack' assignment briefs and devise strategies to meet the marking criteria. Make past papers and exemplar answers widely available
Encourage reflection	Survey students early on to establish prior knowledge, approaches to study, perceptions of education and expectations of university. Use summary results to generate whole-class discussion. Relate findings to 'success skill' statements, employability etc. Build individual reflection into assessment/ feedback through 'learning diaries', reflective essays, personal profile development

Students: intellectual and personal development

A key formative challenge in first year teaching is to help students learn how to behave intelligently and with confidence, when faced with new and difficult subject matter. To an extent students have a responsibility to make use of academic challenges to enhance their analytical and creative powers. However, as many lecturers will attest, this does not always happen, and in fact many incoming students seem to display a distinct preference for having the lecturer package all relevant material in the form of powerpoint slides available for download!

Perhaps this transition issue can be addressed if we make it explicit as one of the key formative challenges in first year and introduce requisite activities as part of the successful completion of first year transition. This would involve lecturers in articulating the kinds of intellectual practices required for higher study in their disciplines and devising student activities to make those practices explicit in the curriculum. For examples, see Table 3.4.

Table 3.4   Student development in practice

Intellectual practices	Examples of student activity from practice
Curiosity, openness to new ideas and willingness to listen to other views	Brainstorming, formulating questions, investigating relevant information, carrying out sustained inquiry work, discussing ideas with peers and lecturers. Acknowledging diversity and including all points of view
Scepticism and critical awareness of the need to gather data, information and present evidence	Asking focused questions, checking sources, keeping detailed notes of practical work. Identifying mistakes and improving performance
Communication which is concise, accurate and persuasive	Devising models, making analogies and comparisons, categorizing information, focusing on key questions, recognizing audience needs and academic conventions. Utilizing a variety of communication technologies. Resisting the temptation to plagiarize

It would be unreasonable to expect incoming students to display all of these characteristics within weeks of joining the academic community. Consequently this is an area of the first year curriculum which will benefit from a carefully articulated process of making the expectations transparent and embedding generative activities progressively in teaching over the year. This is also a prime focus for feedback and assessment strategies, since one of the major gains for students will be to improve their performance in assessments. In addition, these powerful intellectual practices require operational competence in:

- goal setting, planning, managing time, scheduling work, information searching, collaborating with others;
- persisting, overcoming problems, combatting disengagement and disorganization, maintaining focus and self-control;
- increasing complex and creative thinking, developing situational awareness and emotional intelligence, reflecting on values and practice.

Consequently there will be benefit in terms of key employability skills as well as academic improvements. Taken together, these points imply a first year experience:

- giving greater emphasis to confidence building and developing student self-efficacy, rather than assuming students will simply 'mature' as learners over time;
- legitimizing difficulties encountered with subject content as material for reflection and change rather than evidence of failure;
- building a community of support amongst the students and staff in a course/department around common intellectual values.

Let us move on to complete the discussion of mainstreaming with reference to the key areas of student learning and assessment.

Learning: a student concordat

Whilst teaching methods may be sound, their degree of effectiveness will be influenced by student behaviour. Students are expected to co-operate and engage in making their transitions effective. Sample items which lecturers can use to encourage students to take more responsibility through the mainstreaming activities described above include:

- accepting a set of public ground rules for being a successful, efficient and effective student, e.g. norms for attendance, punctuality, preparation, paying attention, participation;
- appreciation of academic values, expectations, rigour and practices;
- positive academic and social interaction with peers;
- an effective balance of all aspects of student lifestyle, and a commitment to succeed;
- self-managing tasks, activities and processes;
- collaborating with peers;
- becoming more self-confident and professional in outlook;
- making more effective use of data and information sources in relation to empirical and discipline-specific study;
- deepening subject knowledge together with awareness of the professional and other criteria operating in the job market.

These points are indicative of what might be proposed to make students' responsibility for engagement a tangible reality in their lives. I suggest that any such concordat might best be developed through dialogue with students, perhaps as part of the process of getting course evaluation feedback. It can be a powerful strategy to get students to confront the contribution their own dispositions, motives and actions make to the quality of their learning environment.

Assessment

Student concepts of and approaches to assessment, or 'exams', can represent a concentrated realization of their understanding of learning. Differing student/staff perceptions of the relationships between learning and assessment can be highly problematic. If the staff expectation is that students will answer questions critically, in depth, clearly and reflectively, it is a problem if many students underperform on those expectations. This may be evidenced in student difficulties with responding to questions, selection of information, structure of response etc. If nothing is done to help students overcome these difficulties they will tend to persist and undermine future performance.

In addition, learning tends to be experienced by students as distinct from assignment hand-ins and exams. So there is a powerful tendency to see assignments in terms of deadlines, to be put off, with examinations seen as coming at the 'end' of a course module, when cramming and superficial recall become the order of the day. Both can have the force of a threat, or escape route, rather than providing a sense of motivation and critical focus for deeper learning.

Degree exams have institutional location in rooms, timetables, exam boards and an institutional weight linked to the system of external examiners, which reinforces this displacement of assessment from learning and exacerbates the sense of external threat. Finally the whole business is usually wrapped up in confidentiality about the actual decisions taken, which creates problems for staff and students in having open discussions about assessment and in providing formative feedback on performance. Modern views on teaching and learning (Chapter 2) would argue against such sharp separations between learning, feedback and assessment, and advocate a more integrated relationship.

Assessment must be a key focus for the mainstreaming project. Student response to assessment is therefore an absolutely critical feature of the first year in higher education involving:

- gaps between prior and present knowledge, experience, expectations and realities;
- assumptions about ability;
- expectations about performance;
- initial formation of student identity.

Assessment is usually at the forefront of students' minds, to the extent that the assessment regime can define the course for them. By contrast, exams are a university tradition and an institutional obligation, which may not have been 'thought about' in any depth by lecturers beyond the necessity of providing questions on their contributions to course teaching. This is not a criticism of lecturers, simply an acknowledgement of the pressure of other work and the inevitable routinization of work over time.

Improving assessment

If students are confused by the terminology of assessment, or uncertain about how to go about a particular assignment, their first year experience will be diminished and they may well perform below their potential. If this happens it will store up difficulty for future intellectual development in the discipline, impede skill development and undermine confidence. Time spent clarifying the purpose of assignments and the kind of performance expected is time very well spent. The outcome should be greater clarity about what is expected and how to meet the expectations combined with improved performance and greater academic confidence.

Mainstreaming the FYE would benefit from a well-defined set of principles and practices for assessment which are specific to first year. The most useful current formulation of assessment principles I have discovered derives from the Re-engineering Assessment Practice (REAP) project, a large-scale initiative funded by the Scottish Funding Council and directed by Professor Nicol, involving collaboration across three Scottish universities. The REAP project has involved the redesign and embedding of innovative assessment practices supported by technology within large-cohort first year classes across a wide range of disciplines (www.reap.ac.uk). To that extent, the project could not be more relevant to the FYE. The work reflects the scholarship of assessment and a major research project on assessment in the first year (Nicol and Macfarlane Dick, (2004, 2006). A key outcome is a set of principles and focus questions indicating that good assessment and feedback practice should do the following:

1 **Help to clarify what good performance is (goals, criteria, standards)**
   To what extent do students on your course have opportunities to engage actively with goals, criteria and standards before, during and after an assessment task?
2 **Encourage 'time and effort' on challenging learning tasks**
   To what extent do your assessment tasks encourage regular study in and out of class and deep rather than surface learning?
3 **Deliver high quality feedback information that helps learners to self-correct**
   What kind of teacher feedback do you provide, and in what ways does it help students to self-assess and self-correct?
4 **Provide opportunities to act on feedback (to close any gap between current and desired performance)**
   To what extent is feedback attended to and acted upon by students in your course and, if so, in what ways?
5 **Ensure that summative assessment has a positive impact on learning**
   To what extent are your summative and formative assessments aligned and supportive of the development of valued qualities, skills and understanding?
6 **Encourage interaction and dialogue around learning (peer and teacher–student)**
   What opportunities are there for feedback dialogue (peer and/or tutor–student) around assessment tasks in your course?

7   **Facilitate the development of self-assessment and reflection in learning**
To what extent are there formal opportunities for reflection, self-assessment or peer assessment in your course?

8   **Give choice in the topic, method, criteria, weighting or timing of assessments**
To what extent do students have choice in the topics, methods, criteria, weighting and/or timing of learning and assessment tasks in your course?

9   **Involve students in decision making about assessment policy and practice**
To what extent are students in your course kept informed or engaged in consultations regarding assessment policy decisions?

10   **Support the development of learning groups and communities**
To what extent do your assessment and feedback processes help to encourage social bonding and the development of learning communities?

11   **Encourage positive motivational beliefs and self-esteem**
To what extent do your assessment and feedback processes enhance your students' motivation to learn and be successful?

12   **Provide information to teachers that can be used to help to shape their teaching**
To what extent do your assessment and feedback processes inform and shape your teaching?

This material can be accessed at: www.reap.ac.uk/public/Papers/Transforming%20assessment_DN.pdf.

Whilst teaching, learning and assessment are the key areas to develop the FYE as part of the academic mainstream, several related issues are worth noting as factors in mainstreaming the FYE.

Mainstreaming study skills and information literacy

In the past, deficits in student learning ability tended to be assumed to be due in some measure to underdeveloped study skills, which could be addressed by advising students to get help. There is therefore a substantial body of published advice and guidance on the what and how of study, aimed directly at students, with the intent of helping individuals to improve their study 'skills' and adopt more satisfactory study 'habits'. Universities have also created units staffed by people who specialize in offering individuals and groups of students advice, guidance and practical help in improving their approach to study.

From a mainstreaming perspective there is a counter-argument to the individual deficit model, and that is that traditional teaching does not develop these skill areas, particularly writing, in sufficient detail. This comes about through a combination of assumptions on the part of lecturers about student abilities and a strong tendency not to devote time and attention to these matters in the classroom. The result is that students tend to underperform on their potential due to lack of well-formed skills development linked to their actual curriculum and stage of development at university. The logic of this argument is that all students should experience systematic support with making transitions from pre-university writing to meeting new disciplinary and professional writing expectations. A practical approach to improving the situation at course level is outlined in Figure 3.3 above.

The published study skills advice literature (including that on websites) attempts to give direct guidance to the student in making the learning transition required by entry to higher education, and may still be regarded by many lecturers as adequate to student needs. Undeniably some students do find this material helpful but, if used in isolation, I contend that it is too simplistic to be effective as an avenue for more sophisticated learning development. A major problem is the tendency to posit study in terms of accepted ways of knowing and relatively mechanistic ways of managing particular study tasks which, once mastered, lead inevitably to academic success.

However, a number of recent studies are challenging some of the earlier weaknesses. These texts provide clear representations of the FYE and ready-made examples of activities and tasks which can be adapted to fit local circumstances. These texts offer a rich source of ideas and exercises that might be used by lecturers to develop micro teaching activities as part of a mainstreaming initiative.

Excellent examples include:

- Cottrell (2008): offers sophisticated perspectives on the nature of learning as well as various techniques to improve writing, time management, exam preparation and so forth
- Sinclair (2006): adopts an approach of demystifying the new world of the university, and offers students many useful insights into academic culture and expectations
- Alston *et al.* (2007): provides an up-to-date account of the field of scholarship skills and useful set of case studies

No doubt colleagues will be able to add their own examples to the list.

In addition to the more obvious study skill issues, the advent of internet access to vast information resources challenges the earlier view that a brief 'library orientation' session at the start of first year would equip students for the information needs of study. Ease of access to information aligned with 'cut and paste' approaches to information use has generated very significant concerns over academic honesty and plagiarism. This is an area where lecturers and librarians need to develop close working partnerships to enhance the FYE. University libraries have tended to be regarded as places where students 'go', although there has been a valuable tradition of librarians being invited 'in' to the classroom, to provide direct advice on using the library and its resources.

These days that tradition has morphed into online tutorials and other resources on the internet, and in local virtual learning environments (VLEs). However, librarians should also be able to offer more proactive contributions under the banner of Information Literacy (see Chapter 6), so it would be sensible to consult the library as part of any mainstreaming project, and to explore the growing research literature on information literacy and higher education. Lupton (2004), Edwards (2006) and Bruce *et al.* (2006) summarize literature on information literacy and provide research-based accounts relating it to teaching and learning in higher education.

Helping individual students

The student learning trajectory will vary with circumstances over the year, and despite the best embedded measures to aid transition there may be periods of disorganized and disengaged learning. If this is widespread it may indicate some imbalance in the course design – too many deadlines bunched together, for example – and this will need attention before the next run of the class. For individuals, dysfunction may be linked with pragmatic attempts to satisfy the basic need to 'pass the exams' by adopting inefficient and ineffective approaches to study, possibly exacerbated by some personal crisis.

Inevitably some students will need individual help from lecturers or others in their disciplinary area, perhaps in the role of Personal Tutor or Academic Adviser (Wheeler and Birtles, 1993), for example students who have fallen behind over a semester and are underperforming on their potential at entry. This situation requires proactive follow-up and intervention with students who are demonstrably having academic difficulties. A good example is from a large chemistry class where the lecturer who co-ordinated the first year labs took on this responsibility and discharged it by holding one-hour meetings with underperformers, to discuss the situation and develop a personalized 'study plan' to get them back on track.

The main features of such study consultation sessions are that they:

● take place outside regular classroom meetings;
● are driven by student need and readiness to change;
● provide a safe environment for discussion;
● focus on discrete academic problems/tasks in depth, and with regard for the personal, social, institutional and pedagogical contexts;
● result in a definite plan of action to improve matters, which can be monitored and supported by the lecturer and, if need be, specialist support staff.

Effectiveness derives as much from the lecturer accepting the student, and conveying that acceptance by the quality of listening, genuineness of response and trust building displayed, as from particular suggestions concerning study skills. These qualities are particularly important when the student population is diverse and sensitivity to different backgrounds is needed. A quick way to explore the personal qualities needed for this activity can be to contact colleagues in one of the specialist student services, who may be able to provide a quick 'tutorial' of some tips and tactics.

Your personal profile as a teacher

The literature of teaching and learning in higher education would identify a 'good' lecturer by his or her professionalism as a teacher characterized by:

- appreciation that learning is more a consequence of what students do than lecturer behaviour;
- capacity to deploy various classroom techniques aimed at encouraging student learning activity;
- ability to evaluate and redesign courses to develop more conducive learning environments;
- willingness to devise effective feedback systems and focus assessment as part of teaching aimed at encouraging depth of learning;
- commitment to building student capacity for self-regulation and facility in group learning processes;
- commitment to scholarship and research on teaching and learning.

Is that you? If not, don't worry too much, as such accomplished performance is unlikely to emerge overnight after quickly reading a selection of the papers suggested in Chapter 2. Consequently it makes more sense to acknowledge the need to be pragmatic about what can and can't be done in the short term, and how you might ensure that your efforts are rewarded. This is particularly so if your colleagues are less than supportive, and more intent on boosting the department's research profile than building a reputation for excellence in first year teaching, or even adopting some of the mainstreaming ideas detailed in this chapter.

In these circumstances I would suggest an approach based on an idea of engaging a good majority of the students in your classes. Their engagement might be characterized as them developing, if not a passion for the subject, at least a sense of its relevance, a desire to find out more and the confidence to go about that enterprise in a competent manner. This position can be operationalized using a limited number of relatively straightforward classroom techniques, such as those indicated above, and, if possible, an extension of feedback effort aimed at improving assessment performance. If over time this strategy leads to you being acknowledged as an effective teacher, and somebody to be listened to at department and faculty teaching committees, then you will be in a stronger position to influence decisions which might lead to more elaborate course redesign.

Building your teaching profile

I would also suggest that you involve some colleagues as you gain more confidence. They might be involved as 'critical friends' who could be relied on to spend some time discussing what you are trying to achieve, perhaps on a basis of shared reading of a relevant paper, and later by observing one of your classes and providing constructive comments. If you are a probationary lecturer then it seems evident to call on colleagues for help, and if you are more experienced it may be that your approach should be seen as a desire to enhance your performance.

In addition you could engage in some action research by investigating student perceptions of the procedure, and perhaps also analysing the impact of your techniques on pass rates and levels of attainment. This might in turn generate changes in the forms of assessment, or the introduction of technologies like Personal Response Systems, sometimes referred to as electronic voting or 'clickers' (Nicol and Boyle, 2003; Banks, 2006; Nicol and Milligan, 2006). It is increasingly possible to obtain funds to support pedagogical research, for example departmental or institutional funding for initiatives linked to educational strategy. However, you should consider external funding at some stage, and look to bodies like the Higher Education Academy (HEA) in the UK, the Australian Learning and Teaching Council (ALTC) and the many charitable bodies in the USA.

Taken in combination these measures can be developed as an exercise in your personal development as a teacher and used to evidence that development, perhaps via a portfolio. This can in turn be deployed whenever your teaching comes up at annual review or other scrutiny. Whilst there is still a strong bias towards research criteria as decisive factors in many academic careers, it seems clear that the changes wrought by massification, diversity and demands for employability attributes will force teaching higher up the institutional agenda.

As this happens the decision-making structures for educational matters will become more important and middle management roles such as Vice Dean Academic will become more prominent. These changing circumstances will require greater expertise in the theory and practice of university teaching as a prerequisite for appointment to such posts. My own view is that the heads of academic departments should be a particular focus of expertise in teaching, including the FYE, given their responsibility for courses and students taking those courses, and their accountability to the university for the quality of education on offer in their areas.

Support for educational development: a model of institutional practice

The last three decades have seen the establishment of specialist departments in universities to assist educational development by providing initial and continuing training and development for lecturers. Some units also carry out research and collaborate with academics in mounting curriculum development projects in their courses. In addition, national organizations such as the HEA in the UK and the ALTC in Australia have been created to encourage and nurture good educational practice in higher education. External quality audit and enhancement of educational provision is now well established as a means of public accountability for funding, and a powerful stimulant for improving teaching practice. Taken together these internal units and external bodies can provide a supportive context for educational development in universities. However, it is up to the institution to provide a supportive context of policy and resource allocation.

The model of educational development I have in mind is a practical and systematic way for lecturers to think about courses and learning experiences, relating course design, teaching, assessment and feedback to student learning. Personal and collegial reflection alongside more formal course evaluations are integral parts of this model. It is not restricted to individuals, or small groups of like-minded colleagues. Indeed, I believe that departmental and institutional support is essential to driving and sustaining successful practice. I also believe that if such support is absent, or less than wholehearted, then the chances of successful educational development are very greatly reduced.

Educational development and the FYE

First, as student numbers have increased and their backgrounds become more diverse, educational development work can be focused on managing the pedagogical implications of these changes to ensure student engagement and success. This would include the institutional headline issue of retention, which can be construed as a proxy term for the issues raised by massification and wider access. Other institution-wide themes are relevant, for example employability, personal development planning and research teaching links. All should be addressed from a basis in pedagogical principle and research-based practice as aspects of mainstream teaching and learning.

Second, the impact of the internet and digital technology demands intelligent direction and a thoughtful approach, which avoids the pitfalls of overemphasizing the technological 'wow' factor. This is a major challenge, given the immense cultural power of discourses which combine technology with 'invention', 'innovation', 'development' and visions of boundless progress, thereby setting professional and institutional agendas in those terms and perhaps clouding alternative viewpoints in the process (Edgerton, 2008).

Finally, there are insistent demands on higher education for greater economic relevance, which may seem like demands to squeeze more out of scarce academic resources. How do lecturers schooled in their disciplines set about the business of embedding 'key skills' and 'employability' in their first year courses and degree programmes? Do they wash their hands of the matter, and leave it to Career Service professionals? Do they make limited changes in their teaching, perhaps by 'bolting on' workshops or professional development-type units? Or do they engage with more complex concepts and practice in-depth and long-term course development (Johnston and Watson, 2006)?

The central services: complementary contributions

Universities have a tradition of central service provision to meet FYE needs, with relatively unstructured support via the curriculum. In addition, institutions will need to assure prospective students, their families and sector quality agencies that these needs will be met. If an academic mainstreaming model is adopted and grafted onto the earlier tradition, this should be treated as an opportunity for new partnerships between academic and service professionals based on a shared commitment to the FYE. A brief summary of some of the main features of modern service provision will complement the account of mainstreaming. Key features of the central services approach are:

- services resourced to operate as a catch-all for the students in difficulty;
- services aspiring to contribute to the well-being and development of all students.

Their key commitment is likely to be to at-risk groups and those students who need individual solutions to personal and financial problems and difficulties arising from disability. They are also likely to place a high premium on contributing to the success of widening access programmes and recruitment generally. The specialist knowledge required to respond to these complex issues should not be expected from academics, so there is a fundamental and ongoing role for central service units and their staff.

Characteristics of the central services model

The following concerns and approaches describe the modern central services model.

- Aim of promoting and co-ordinating an integrated induction and transition programme for all students
- Acceptance of transition, formation, engagement, empowerment and participation as key support service themes
- Central units staffed by professionals – counsellors, financial advisers, learning advisers, special needs advisers, careers advisers etc.

- Mixed provision of general advisory and guidance services, with personal service to individuals

Clearly the levels of staffing and resources directed to these matters will vary, and it is a reasonable guess that few service directors and their staff will accept that resource provision could not be improved.

Central service development agendas

Proposed major strategic agendas for the central services might include:

- more integrated organizational structures;
- 'one stop shop' premises;
- increased staffing, including staff dedicated to FYE work;
- greater liaison and co-operation with academics.

The first two points are likely to be a significant focus of strategic effort in the institution as they relate directly to the public profile of the institution and the capacity to make a valuable contribution to the student life cycle. However, service professionals may vary in the degree of confidence they have in the practicality of changing the academic attitudes and commitment required by university-wide mainstreaming of the FYE as part of the curriculum. Nevertheless, the services provide a solid bulwark of student-centred support for the FYE in their institutions and should be drawn into any FYE enhancement initiative. Their perspectives on the student experience and their knowledge of arcane matters like student finance are invaluable.

Mainstreaming – a note of realism

I do not suggest that these ideas are revolutionary, simply that they should contribute to giving more students a smoother academic transition and encourage more students to become more engaged with their courses. However, I believe that if these approaches were to be adopted in policy, applied consistently across a whole department and given sustained institutional support, the result would be an improved baseline experience for all incoming students. That would be a very great gain for all concerned in that institution. Therefore institutional monitoring might be required to focus activity and monitor consistency at departmental and course level. Three linked strategies to boost mainstreaming are worth considering:

- A checklist of mainstream transition activities based in the items detailed above, circulated to all Heads of Departments by the Vice Chancellor prior to the start of each first year, requiring the Head of Department (HoD) to sign off that each item is a live facet of the FYE in their area

- Faculty/school monitoring of the quality of mainstream activity on the FYE in every class, with a specific annual report to Senate and Council/ Court during each academic year
- Where pass rates and student progression data arising from first year classes are scrutinized by faculty/school/senate committees, a specific account of the operation of mainstream activities should be required for every class/course which is below the relevant pass rate benchmark

However, the real long term significance of having a consistent baseline may lie in the fact that it will identify the options for enhancement, by targeting educational and organizational development much more accurately at approaches that might enhance the FYE above the basic levels of pedagogical transparency. This will be the subject of Chapter 4.

Conclusions

I suggested two interrelated approaches to the FYE in this chapter:

- academic mainstreaming;
- central service model.

These approaches are not mutually exclusive. In practice they are complementary; the question is one of balance between them. Traditionally the central services approach has been assumed to be the best option to address the FYE; however, my view is that in a period of 'mature' mass higher education, it is inadequate without a new approach to students' academic experiences. Hence my emphasis on the need to place the FYE in the mainstream of academic activity, with pedagogical measures to address transition in the foreground of courses. Equally, institutions should be taking advantage of changed circumstances to carry out large-scale course development whenever possible.

4

Course design for FYE: a case study

Introduction

Chapters 1–3 highlight the importance of the FYE as a distinctive pedagogical unit in the curriculum and suggest that measures to support students in transition should be integrated with mainstream teaching in all first year classes. This chapter develops these analytic themes by introducing a *case study* as a logical extension of the mainstreaming approach described in Chapter 3.

This case study of a major curriculum renewal project demonstrates how an approach grounded in pedagogical principles can be turned into a viable and sustainable course design. The case study represents an exercise in large-scale curriculum renewal from first year onwards which began in the late 1990s. The strategic aim was to integrate student learning in business studies, and address government and graduate employer demands for work-related skills as described in the Dearing Report (National Committee of Enquiry into Higher Education, 1997). The FYE in this case was underpinned by perspectives seen as critical to successful transition in the first year and student activity was scaffolded by explicit measures embedded in teaching practice.

For example, students were engaged with learning through substantial collaborative team project work and early feedback on their skills as writers and presenters was emphasized. The level of difficulty and responsibility was increased progressively over the year and student performance was closely monitored to support effective transition. Students were required to spend time reflecting on their experiences, supported by feedback on their written accounts of reflection. The course design was based in current pedagogical principles and implemented by staff collaborating as a teaching team, with regular meetings to share experience and fine tune activity.

Towards guided independence: a case study

The class in this case study forms part of the Business BA at Strathclyde University Business School (SBS). It is a compulsory three-year programme for all business students involving approximately five hundred students each year at present. The programme embraces:

- confidence building;
- personal effectiveness;
- management skills, leadership and negotiation;
- social, ethical and sustainability issues in business;
- professional values and project management.

Integration of this complex and demanding set of elements is the desired outcome of study and provided the class with its original title of Integrative Studies (Belton *et al.*, 2001). Subsequent evaluation and development of the programme resulted in a change of title to the Management Development Programme (MDP) (Johnston and Watson, 2006).

How then was integration to be initiated, sustained and developed through the learning strategy and teaching practice of a large class of new and diverse undergraduates? The following discussion relates to the start-up period in 1999/2000.

Guiding principles

Three key pedagogical principles to enhance the experience of learning can be identified to define and explain the reasoning behind the various educational practices entailed in the case study. Arguably all three principles can be applied to any large first year course to increase the likelihood of achieving a healthy balance between development of student autonomy and social confidence in the learning situation, whilst reducing problems of passivity and alienation. Achieving such a balance would enable significant extension of the academic expectations that might be pursued in subsequent years, but would require some specific course design constructs to ensure degree programme coherence and systematic nurturing of the developing sense of academic independence and social competence. To simplify usage I will term this learning strategy *guided independence*.

- **Learning for understanding**: Replacing the notion that learning is mainly about memorization and test preparation with a concept that prizes complex cognitive activity and encourages interaction between cognition, social involvement and motivation when devising learning experiences – thus encouraging intellectually complex and socially challenging approaches to study by students
- **Teaching for learning**: Replacing the model of the lecturer as primarily a transmitter of disciplinary knowledge and examiner of student comprehension with a model that seeks to improve student learning and

adjustment by moving the student – personified as actively and confi-
dently taking responsibility for developing robust understanding – to the
centre of the educational stage. In this model the lecturer's role is
characterized as organizer and facilitator of learning situations and
provider of timely feedback on student development.

- **Development for lecturers**: Recognition that pedagogical change is
  complex, time-consuming and evolutionary, and that change in the
  higher education context should involve lecturers not only developing a
  more facilitative style of teaching but also adopting a scholarship-based
  and research-oriented educational practice.

In essence the three principles can be viewed as a practical distillation of the
pedagogical and educational development ideas outlined in Chapter 2.
Hopefully this will provide an example of how ideas from the literature can
be translated into guiding principles for practice.

Teaching, learning and assessment: teams and projects

We sought to implement the strategy of *guided independence* as follows:

- By instituting *teams of between six and eight students as the basic educational
  unit as opposed to several hundred individual learners*, thereby immediately
  challenging the alienation of traditional course designs, encouraging
  social interaction and placing the focus firmly on collaboration and
  interpersonal skill development
- By *making team projects the central feature of assessment and by devising team
  projects that focus on business problems* (performance measurement and
  forecasting in first semester; establishing the market for a particular
  product in semester two). Projects required: group participation, planning and time management; practical research using data sets, internet
  and electronic library; production of business reports and preparation
  and delivery of oral presentations, incorporating statistical techniques
  and using relevant information technology. Having two relatively small
  scale projects in first semester allowed students to: get to know each
  other and the staff; gain experience of team working; and receive early
  feedback and assessment of performance
- By providing a *weekly blend of:* labs (1–2 hours) in computing, information
  technology and statistical techniques with student project teams timeta-
  bled together; whole-class plenary sessions (1 hour) and tutor facilitated
  team meetings (1 hour) to provide information, guidance and training
  and allow scheduling of mini-presentations of team work in progress; a
  class website, updated weekly, containing all the relevant information
  about the class organization, lab worksheets, plenary points; invited

speakers from business explaining their organization's approaches to the team project topics. The teaching style and forms of staff/student contact stressed interaction, informality and staff approachability

- By *involving the whole class in decisions about content and process through feedback and dialogue,* partly through ongoing discussion in the course of teaching but formally through a variation of classroom assessment (Angelo and Cross, 1993) carried out in a plenary session mid-way through first semester. Each student was asked to write views on the class on index cards together with suggestions for improvement and the cards were collected and analysed
- By *getting students to reflect on their individual aspirations, experiences in groups, achievements, strengths, weaknesses and areas for further development through an assessed learning diary, comprising:* review of progress between team projects; general essay on the integrative experience; checklist of all skill areas with specific examples to encourage systematic and periodic review of individual progress in all areas. The diary was submitted for assessment and feedback at the end of each semester, so students have two rounds of systematic reflection and feedback.
- By *organizing the staff as a combined course design and teaching team.* The team met weekly and comprised lecturers from management science, information science, economics and statistics, supported by graduate teaching assistants. I worked with the team from an educational development and evaluation perspective, contributed to some whole-class sessions and also facilitated and assessed a number of student teams. The class was managed by a professor reporting to the faculty, and there was a part-time administrator (in due course a senior lecturer devoted half of her time to take on the role of programme manager)
- *Accommodation included*: lecture room with whole-class capacity; adjacent rooms to allow a degree of flow between large plenary meetings and smaller gatherings of teams; bookable computer labs and a class office. Teaching team meetings were held weekly to review progress, plan ahead and evolve the class through our observations of student activity; team 'marking' sessions were held to ensure validity and consistency of assessment and to develop shared understandings

The student experience of integrative studies: observations, feedback and learning diaries

This account draws on student feedback gathered from the whole class, insight drawn from a sample of individual student learning diaries and staff observations.

Orientation and early adjustment: student feedback

The following summary of student feedback (data collected on index cards during whole-class meeting in mid-semester one) gives a flavour of students' early responses to the learning environment.

- Staff approachable and responsive to students
- Early anxiety over expectations e.g. first team project
- Criticism of performance management as a topic choice – too abstract
- Website useful and user-friendly
- Labs practical with helpful tutors and worksheets
- Teams a valuable way of developing interpersonal skill and getting to know people; more time should be given to teams, less to whole-class sessions
- Some calls for more control and guidance by lecturers
- Involvement of outside business representatives generally welcomed

We fed these points back to the whole class and collaboratively agreed more time for team working in second semester, thereby encouraging students to share responsibility for teaching decisions with us and each other. Making the change to more team working sooner would have compromised aspects of the class schedule for the rest of semester one, and we also felt it prudent to give students more time to settle in and get feedback on performance in teams before increasing their autonomy and self-management responsibilities. This approach acknowledged the various anxieties present in the class and recognized that students were also having to cope with four other first year classes. It also provided valuable data for subsequent course management around the issue of mediating dependence, independence and student self-reliance both in semester two and looking ahead to Session 2001/02.

The feedback confirmed our observations that students were finding some aspects of the environment a source of anxiety and frustration; however, they were clearly in favour of working in teams and being consulted about their opinions. These early weeks were a period of balancing the development of student confidence in each other and in staff's willingness to listen and respond to them, whilst moving the class towards the team projects, reports and presentations that constituted their assessment. In general terms, performance on the first project displayed some weaknesses in understanding, team working and communication. However, project two showed marked improvement and the small number of teams required to repeat either project displayed significant improvement in confidence and results.

Engagement and independence: teams and diaries

The following section draws on a sample of 25 student learning diaries completed after semester one, thereby entailing review of all the learning experiences. The diaries formed part of assessment and required students to write within a template that they download from the class website. The diary contained sections for students to: state their incoming aspirations for the class, review the first two team projects, write a short general essay on how the class had met their aspirations and systematically self-assess progress in all key skills areas. In most cases the students' reflections went beyond simple reactive accounts to encompass: self-assessment, discussion of problems in team working and proposed solutions. The following points represent recurring themes across the sample diaries:

- Teams regarded as the most valuable aspect of the class and portrayed as participation, communication, planning to divide labour and provide mutual support at oral presentations
- Ability to listen to others cited as an important and unexpected aspect of team management
- Teams also regarded as valuable opportunity to meet other people and reduce sense of isolation in a new environment
- Difficulties in planning and co-ordinating projects acknowledged and better time management identified as a solution
- Value of skills to future employment stressed and relevance of team and presentation skills to other classes acknowledged
- Mixed evaluation of benefits of computing labs depending on student estimate of their level of prior expertise

The writing displayed in the diaries was a blend of concise project description and discursive account of how far aspirations had been met. In general the diaries showed students growing in confidence and ability to self-assess and take responsibility for performance and performance improvement.

The three educational principles revisited: independence and support in first year

Of the three principles, the first two (learning and teaching) had most obvious direct impact on the problem of student autonomy and support through the interaction of: teams; team projects; facilitative teaching; and reflective learning diaries to encourage evolving student independence. The two team projects in first semester required students to exercise a degree of independent and co-ordinated action to research, write up and orally present their account of a business problem, whilst the diaries encouraged individuals to recall and reflect on the experience. Students had to take responsibility for identifying and assessing the strengths and weaknesses of their team working and suggest ways to improve performance and avoid difficulties.

Social engagement and peer support were engendered by the experience of teams both as a training ground in group dynamics, task management and mutual support and as a valuable opportunity to meet a manageable number of new people who could form part of the student's friendship group and social life outside the class. Teams also encouraged staff/student dialogue, live and by email, and offered a gateway to personal advice, support and, where relevant, reference to university support services. Dependence on lecturers as the sole source of information and learning was reduced and more independent modes of working encouraged in a situation where lecturer support could be sought, particularly in terms of problem interpretation as opposed to simple repetition of information from lectures. Teaching was in effect operating as a form of guided independence rather than a 'lecturer transmits information/students sink or swim in that sea of information' model.

The third principle (staff development) enabled the other two by helping staff to adopt and adapt interactive and facilitative approaches to teaching through regular discussion of observations, identification and resolution of problems and mutual support and encouragement. In practice, whilst the teaching team meetings required discussion of week-by-week activity, those discussions presented as decision-making debates over how best to mediate student understanding, motivation and performance in the light of student feedback and our observations of student activity. This collaborative process has been a very powerful form of staff development through action, in that issues of practice and educational theory have been synthesized through the actions and reflections of team members.

Summation

There is no suggestion that the course design and pedagogical practice described in this case study offers a final blueprint for first year curricula. Indeed, the course has grown and developed over the ensuing decade and has been retitled the Management Development Programme. This process of educational development is detailed in Johnston *et al.*, 2002; Johnston and Watson, 2004, 2006. In terms of developing a mainstream approach to the FYE, this experience has shown what can be done in a particular degree programme, in one institution.

Generalizing the case study

Here are my reflections on the case study in relation to the FYE. Distilling the experience into some general guiding principles involves:

- devising a statement of higher order factors;
- integration of FYE within whole-of-degree programmes;
- a framework for institutional management of the curriculum;
- four principles/practices of strategic curriculum review.

When linked together and backed by serious institutional commitment, these components should channel energy and time efficiently and effectively.

Higher order factors

These are the influencers which can be used to audit existing practice and suggest areas for improvement. My own distillation of the knowledge in the field of FYE inquiry is expressed in term of five higher order items:

- Congruence – do student expectations and experiences 'fit'?
- Genuineness – are staff/students committed?
- Curriculum – is there systematic educational provision for transition?
- Resource – is there a specific budget?
- Leadership – is there an academic locus?

These points should help focus strategic thinking on the most important conditions to be met in creating successful courses renewal.

Integration of FYE within whole-of-degree programmes

I surmise that the *degree programme* framework focuses aspects of first year teaching and curriculum development that have received somewhat less attention in many universities. The following components identify practical curriculum renewal activities:

- design of course units;
- team teaching.

Design of course units

I offer not an exact blueprint but an educational design and development approach that can be interpreted and developed to match institutional circumstances. The framework can be used as an analytical tool for researchers, teachers, strategic and other managers to address curricular facets and relationships. The *course/unit level* framework will be familiar to higher educators, and should be embedded in institutional procedures requiring detailed course descriptions to permit decisions to introduce new courses etc. This systematic model of course design concentrates on the design, description, management and evaluation of particular credit-bearing courses in terms of questions about the following:

- **Course rationale**: discipline, pedagogy and market place factors determining the introduction of a new course/renovation of an existing course. The transition issues described in Chapter 1 would provide a source of FYE-specific items e.g. increased enrolments, diversity, preparation for study, retention issues, employability
- **Course aims and objectives**: disciplinary content, student learning strategy, generic features e.g. graduate attributes. The issues, ideas and measures discussed in Chapters 1 and 2 offer specific terminology to express objectives e.g. engagement, empowerment
- **Course design**: teaching, learning and assessment of student achievement; student learning strategy; staff approach to teaching and assessment. Chapter 3 and the foregoing case study provide indicative descriptions and concrete examples of practice
- **Staffing, accommodation, resources and infrastructure:** opportunities, constraints and estate/accommodation management
- **Evaluation and improvement of quality** over time, including student and other stakeholder feedback. University-wide collection of data on the FYE would inform decision-making bodies

This framework can be viewed as a general systems tool for decision taking about designing, developing and managing courses irrespective of the mode of attendance and media formats involved. I suspect that a variation of this model will be familiar to many educational developers, learning technologists and lecturers (Rowntree, 1982; Biggs, 2007).

Team teaching

My experience of large-scale course projects is that a design and delivery team is essential, ideally guided by a smaller strategic development group. This smaller group would treat the curriculum renewal project holistically, propose theoretically informed designs, evaluate effectiveness, research teaching and learning, present and publish findings in professional forums and in academic publications. Regular 'away days' pre- and post-session, dedicated to in-depth reflection and forward planning, are an efficient and effective way to build the team, induct new members, refine the course design and build cases to advocate for increased resources etc.

As team members leave and take on new teaching responsibilities there can be dissemination of experiences and pedagogical ideas to other courses and institutions. As careers develop there can be a similar effect of introducing ideas and criteria based on experience to academic decision-making forums, resource allocations and new staff appointments.

Integration of FYE within whole-of-degree programmes: a common framework

In the UK perhaps the most pervasive form of large-scale innovation in the last twenty years has been the adoption of modular course structures. This process has typically been justified in terms of expanding student choice and now provides the structural context for both disciplinary programmes and cross-curricular initiatives in most institutions. However, in order to extract the optimum benefit from a programme of study towards a degree some attention must be paid to academic integrity and overall programme coherence. The formative role of first year should receive particular attention in its own right and in relation to progression pathways.

This requires a common frame of reference to guide programme management at institutional levels and provide transparency in programme description, to support student choice. In essence it should be clear to students from the outset how their degree programme is structured and the extent of choice they have. Equally, where a course description promises a particular emphasis between practical/theoretical work, for example, that promise should be delivered.

I suggest four primary organizing constructs to identify, explain and influence the extent of *integration and co-ordination* within a whole degree programme. These constructs have relevance to discussions regarding particular modules, but would have the added value of focusing discussion at both departmental and faculty/school of study levels on the relationship between modules and year(s) of study. Clearly a systematically designed degree programme would be able to demonstrate how transition, engagement and formative assessment, for example, enabled and empowered students to progress successfully through the degree and achieve all its objectives.

The four categories in Table 4.1 represent categories of analysis/description for whole degree programmes. Arguably the academic coherence of a degree could be accounted in terms of statements about how the categories frame the programme and how particular sequences of classes are aligned to construct the degree and define pathways within the programme.

Table 4.1 Integration and co-ordination of whole degree programmes

Analytical categories	Applied to	Key questions
1 Breadth, depth, balance, relevance	Decisions about content, cross-curricular elements, and student experience in terms of subjects, attitudes, vocational relevance	How are the four categories blended in a given curriculum, to ensure sufficient attention to each of them? What is emphasized/ marginalized? What is compulsory, optional, elective?
2 Continuity within the whole programme of study	Subject stages, year on year and within years. Interdisciplinary studies. Cross-curricular issues	How is continuity represented to students e.g. 'steps and stairs', 'spiral'?
3 Progression over time	Any levels identified within subjects e.g. foundation, intermediate, advanced. Also levels of learning e.g. surface/deep, familiarity/mastery, understanding/critical appreciation. Degree of control over processes e.g. passive/active, internal/external locus of control	What prerequisites are required for entry to a programme? What prerequisites are assumed? How are the different kinds of progression acknowledged, taught, assessed? What requirements are imposed to permit formal progression from one stage to the next?
4 Differentiation and variety of the learning community	Individual and group differences in background, experience, expectations, disposition, motivation, application, progress and achievement. Variation in teaching practice, assessment and other pedagogical factors	How far is diversity acknowledged in the curriculum? What is the extent of student choice in constructing learning paths? Do lecturers explain their decisions to choose one teaching/ assessment practice over another?

Analysis implies change and development of curriculum, and this requires some practical guidance.

Four principles/practices of strategic curriculum review

Turning now to the practical business of curriculum review. All four analytical categories can be applied to analysis and management of FYE, to ensure that FYE issues and transition are valued and addressed in all of their degree programmes. In addition such a review would ensure that the FYE explicitly laid the foundations for subsequent academic success and attainment of graduate attributes as a crucial part of lifelong learning.

I suggest that to achieve this, institutions adopt an approach to strategic curriculum review aimed at assuring that the academic integrity of their programmes are qualified by certain essential strategic requirements (see Table 4.2).

Table 4.2   Strategic curriculum review in practice

Strategic requirements	Practices to ensure coherence and integrity of first year curriculum within the degree programme
1 Disciplinary content revised periodically to incorporate new knowledge and address new social, economic and cultural circumstances	Additional knowledge is compensated by removing or de-emphasizing some older material; teaching practice is reviewed to ensure that student workload is not adversely affected; effectiveness of pedagogy in maximizing student engagement is evaluated alongside content review
2 Intellectual development emphasized by reviewing accounts of cognitive, personal and interpersonal growth	Identification of how disciplines add progressively to intellectual development, particularly in relation to first year curricula; embedding and assessing student development in terms of research skills, information literacy, graduate attributes, communication, ethical understanding and citizenship

3 Student engagement and empowerment highlighted at all levels of the curriculum	Compulsory, elective and optional parts of degree programmes regulated to reduce constraints and increase choice of pathways; the overall mix of these parts and their horizontal and vertical connections should be explicit and subject to detailed academic advising; teaching practice should be co-ordinated across programmes to ensure an integrated learning experience from first year onwards
4 Pedagogies adopted as the most suited to encouraging learning in relation to knowledge and also social and cultural circumstances	Disciplinary pedagogies should be compared and debated in relation to perceived best practices, empirical research and coherent bodies of research literature; the specific work on the FYE should be referenced in practice; teaching should be organized from a base in informed discussion, implying a more collective approach; career paths for teaching should be explicit and have parity with other activities such as research

Conclusions

However, what of institutional commitment? I will explore this question in detail in Chapter 5. In the meantime, Wimshurst and Allard (2008), reporting an empirical study of 'academic failure' in their institution, found, not surprisingly, that first year students were more at risk than others. They concluded by emphasizing the need to direct institutional resources to protect first year students from risk of academic failure and enhance their chances of success.

> Such a focusing of resources would indicate a commitment by institutions to engaging students from the start. To government, it would also indicate the commitment by institutions to meeting performance indicators that measure student retention and academic progress. (Wimshurst and Allard, 2008: 697)

I chose this quote from their paper to round off this chapter, because it poses the institutional challenge very directly in terms of the external environment that influences higher education. These seem to me to be powerful arguments for resourcing an approach to bring FYE into the academic mainstream and engage with the kind of in-depth, long-term curriculum renewal described in the foregoing case study. The idea of such *organizational alignment* uniting pedagogy, academic strategy and business process is raised by this comprehensive approach. The next chapter sets out an institutional dimension which can act as a vehicle for curriculum renewal and staff development across the institution.

5

Institutional strategy and the first year experience

Introduction

In this chapter I want to advance the notion that good practice in the FYE has as much to do with the behaviour of senior university leaders as it does with the actions of students and lecturers. Without the wholehearted and informed contributions of management in allocating resources and rewarding effort, it is difficult to see how the FYE can be sustained and enhanced for all students. Leadership must take form in a realistic plan of action for the FYE which encompasses both academic strategy and business process and replaces unsystematic, piecemeal approaches.

To achieve this position, institutions will need to dedicate planning time and management authority to the FYE. They will also need to ensure that strategic activity to develop the FYE is a genuine force for change and does not become a bureaucratic exercise substituting for action. It is in this spirit that I treat strategic 'action plans' as tangible assets for a university, which convey ways of thinking about organizational development, and in this case educational development, rather than being targets for scepticism and cynicism.

The preceding chapters allow us to define the FYE in various ways, and I have attempted to sketch a developmental trajectory which progresses through provision based in central services and the efforts of some committed individual lecturers, through an account of an enhanced role for teachers of first year classes, leading to advocacy of course renewal. The main responses to have evolved, as I see them, can be distilled as:

- generalized transition programmes and associated central services;
- mainstreaming first year and transition measures in courses and renewing course designs.

Armed with these broad perspectives it should be possible for an institution to decide a strategy to enhance the FYE for its students, in ways which align with other institutional priorities and circumstances. Clearly the FYE strategy for an Oxford or Sydney is likely to differ significantly from a Napier or Charles Sturt, simply because of their very different histories and current situation. This does not mean that the FYE in a given institution is immutable. External pressures can force change, as can a major internal review and remodelling of the whole university, such as that currently in progress at the University of Melbourne. The best outcome for a university would be to offer all its students a powerful first year of effective and consistent social and academic engagements to support transition and empower them to get the most out of university.

However, 'on paper' planning exercises are not enough to ensure change. Enhancement depends on both the content of the FYE action plan and how far staff motivation and reward are refocused on FYE specific structures, measures and activities. As many colleagues will know, it is relatively easy to develop a new 'system' for first year on paper, but harder to implement change throughout the institution. My intention with this chapter is to provide some insights and tools which may bring the 'plan' and the 'practice' into closer alignment to the benefit of students, staff and the institution.

Organizational development of the FYE

This chapter will deal with how institutions might reconceptualize the FYE and bring about organizational development by changing policy, strategies, infrastructure and resource allocations. The chapter will also tackle the realistic concern that factors such as underfunding of HE budgets, and the pressures of research selectivity on staff, may lead to any significant change in a university's approach to the FYE being seen as a 'risky shift'. The conceptual changes and organizational tensions involved in making such shifts in activity and culture are likely to be very challenging. Consequently the following framework elements are aimed at easing the process by clarifying thinking and focusing decisions.

Change on any significant scale may have to be measured in years of institutional activity, rather than the weeks and months of focused, project-based activity which have defined much developmental work in the past. Effective, tangible change is also likely to require a reconfiguration of academic staff activity, motives and values – a refixing of the 'rate' for the job, as it were. In others words, institutional leaders need to go through a process of *local* definition, costing and strategic development of FYE enhancement.

The chapter falls into three main sections:

- A framework of ideas and tools to help reconceptualize the FYE as a management issue and focus of organizational development
- A set of key moves to allow phasing and timing of strategy development
- A distillation of principles and intentions into a framework and checklist of actions

In short, this chapter will treat the discussion of FYE as a worked example of how organizational development and academic strategy might be combined. Hopefully this will be useful to all parties with a stake in university governance and management.

I have tried to avoid as far as possible writing in management speak, in order to engage a more general audience of colleagues. For myself, I find university organizational structures and power plays endlessly fascinating, if periodically infuriating. This is an attitude developed over many years of involvement, with some successes and as many disappointments, supplemented by much discussion with colleagues from a variety of universities around the world.

In that spirit I have tried to write for colleagues who want to change institutional policy and practice for the FYE and who are willing to endure the necessary committees and internal politics to do so. I will also suggest how some at least of the organizational delays can be short-circuited. My main objective throughout is to emphasize the importance of keeping tight control over the length of time taken to carry out decision-making processes, without losing the benefits of the institutional research, open discussion and awareness raising required to make substantial and sustainable changes. The framework of tools and mechanisms set out below should help focus awareness, stimulate investigation and support efficient decision making.

In effect this is a chapter written by an actively involved observer of organizational practice, to distil some lessons for the benefit of newcomers and experienced managers alike. Newcomers will hopefully get a sense of how things can be done, and more experienced colleagues may gain some new ways of looking at familiar questions and situations. Whether experienced players or newcomers to the scene, colleagues who find themselves, reluctantly or enthusiastically, involved in the committee structures and associated working groups of their universities form part of what I call the institutional *policy community*. This community provides the means of articulation of ideas and policy between the 'top' level of governance and executive management and the 'middle' and 'bottom' levels of departmental activity.

This is the key group in any institution which channels discussion, questions flawed plans, proposes change and influences decisions at senate or governing body level that will guide the activities of HoDs and staff alike. They may also champion new measures amongst their colleagues in departments and built support for change. Some members of the community will be involved as part of their administrative jobs, others as representatives of their faculties or services, and in all likelihood student representatives will participate in at least some of the activity. This group also have a powerful role in ensuring the university has sound evaluation processes, such as regular quality reporting, and useful practical checklists to assist staff in their activities.

In any case they constitute a significant institutional force which can span the formal and informal organizational structures and ensure that policy and strategy are aligned to the realities of academic life. By their efforts, progress can be significantly advanced and substantial improvements achieved.

A framework to reconceptualize management of the FYE

What has been said so far about the FYE in terms of recruitment, retention, student engagement, empowerment and progression implies that some form of distinctive organizational structure is in place to provide strategic oversight and operational consistency. These days one would be looking for forms going beyond basic academic committee reporting or discussion.

The generic tools for managing major activities like the FYE include:

- organizational structures;
- planning and budgeting processes;
- decision-making bodies;
- management roles;
- staff responsibilities.

All universities will utilize such tools for their activities, but they are unlikely to be organized around the FYE. FYE activity will be scattered across the organization and may not even appear as an item for consideration in the budgeting process, for example. However, many institutions will have utilized enabling processes to develop the FYE. For example, institutional research can be undertaken to provide an evidence base for practice; faculty and department-specific action groups and teams can be formed to focus on the first year; forms of institution-wide development aimed at aligning academic strategy to first year initiatives can be set up. In addition, the FYE is very likely to have featured in initiatives concerned with retention, given that this has been a major concern of governments and sector leaders as massification has developed. In all this, the importance of accessing student opinion, experience and suggestions for improvement cannot be over-emphasized, and will be considered in more detail below.

More specific implementations are now needed to draw FYE matters together and bring them into the focal awareness of decision makers. A starting point is to acknowledge that the FYE encompasses at least eight dimensions of the student life cycle:

   (i)   recruitment, retention and satisfaction;
  (ii)   orientation, induction and adjustment;
 (iii)   course design;
  (iv)   the nature and quality of teaching, learning and assessment;

   (v)   advice, guidance and pastoral care;
   (vi)   administration and co-ordination of programmes and services;
   (vii)   equity and inclusion;
   (viii)   co-curricular opportunities and issues.

Each of these is likely to be embedded in a functional unit, or units, with varying networks of relationship, depending on the extent of centralized or devolved authority in the university. However, it is unlikely that there will be a designated 'unit' for the FYE. For example, there may be a central department responsible for marketing and liaison activities required by (i), with clear channels to academic departments, whereas (iii) is most likely to be managed in academic departments, in line with institutional guidelines and reporting. Equity and inclusion (vii) may be centrally mandated and differentiated by the particular circumstances of courses and degree structures. Clearly co-ordination is an issue, and with the best of intentions it would be no surprise if the FYE did not have the sharpness of focus I have been arguing for.

   Creating a specific organizational structure for FYE activity would require as a minimum networking the units responsible for each of these aspects, and managing their interdependencies. A further development would be to devise a broad but detailed checklist of good practices which could be used across the university to ensure consistency between departments. It would also, I believe, go beyond that to explore the place of the FYE in degree structures and in relation to ideas of lifelong learning, for example.

Reconceptualizing the FYE: tools for review and improvement

I suggest that achieving this degree of coherent organization requires a fundamental rethink of the FYE as an organizational issue, and cannot be achieved within an organizational mindset dominated by piecemeal solutions and loosely connected responsibilities, operating in routine and reactive modes. It is unlikely that existing sub-units, for example, will give up their organizational positions or ways of thinking about the FYE and providing support for transition without such a rethink.

   The following four items (Table 5.1) are the key tools in my suggested approach to reconceptualizing the institutional strategic management of the FYE. Each construct represents a category of strategic thinking about the FYE and suggests practical measures which can be taken to redirect effort. Taken together the constructs emphasize the organizational complexity of the FYE whilst offering greater strategic focus and coherence. They are relevant to any process of review which engages with the idea of the FYE, for example: student retention, student satisfaction, course revision, quality reporting.

Table 5.1   Conceptual tools for strategic development of the FYE

Tools	Rationale
1 Decision-making model	Allows key variables to be manipulated to optimise FYE and fit circumstances and priorities
2 Typology of institutional strategies	Allows broad choice of approach and channelling of decisions
3 Risky shift and rate fixing	Identifies key structural and human resource challenges to be met in implementing strategic decisions
4 Model of institutional dynamics	Connects key aspects and shows relationships between different organizational levels and functions

The constructs are presented in this sequence for convenience, and I am not suggesting that this is a strict hierarchy. It may be more useful for readers to reflect on the constructs and adapt them to best suit local circumstances, perhaps by applying them to the strategic moves outlined below.

A decision-making model: conceptual tool 1

This model combines five key variable factors in a first year strategy which can be used to decide on priority areas for effort. The basic idea is that institutional management of FYE strategy, and aligned activity, can be described by considering how an institution's managers might manipulate the variables in the model to best advantage against local circumstances and in pursuit of institutional change. It is likely that work is undertaken on each factor at present, for example setting targets for student numbers. However, I suspect it is rare for all five factors to be considered in a joined-up fashion in an institution, and this weakness may be compounded by the absence of any one forum for detailed consideration of how the factors relate to each other.

Since the decisions which emerge will reflect wider considerations of institutional priority, positioning and baseline values, this should not be a matter purely for senior managers. All members of the academic community, including students, and indeed external stakeholders such as the state, employers, families and political and other groups with an interest in higher education, should have a say. The following figure seeks to display the mix of business process such as recruitment with academic concerns such as student engagement, whilst identifying five strategic success factors in the same plane as the relevant management tasks. In practice all of these phenomena will be separated at different levels of the organization, and decisions about one may be taken with little awareness of the consequences for the others. Clearly the strategic gain is to consciously manipulate the five factors so that they produce, as far as possible, positive effects on the business and academic processes most relevant to the FYE.

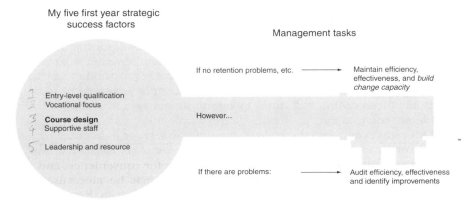

Figure 5.1 Institutional aspects of an excellent first year

Recruitment, retention/progression, engagement/empowerment, success

Factor 1: Competitive entry, high entry qualifications

The most obvious strategic implication for institutions seeking maximum safety and insulation against risk in their student business would be to select students on an elite basis, in order to reduce the possibility of purely academic weaknesses undermining first year performance – in effect to be a university which *selects* its students as opposed to *recruiting* them. Every nation has universities which would be easily recognizable in these terms, and many more universities have particular faculties or specific courses which would be similarly recognized and their places sought after. The objective would be to drive up admission standards in the hope of reducing attrition and increasing successful completion.

Clearly this is not such an easy option in the face of external pressures to widen access, and traditional, elite institutions have been strongly encouraged to change their admissions procedures in order to attract more students from outside their traditional school and social catchments. However, it is difficult to imagine a university with a strong reputation and great pulling power in the student market giving that advantage up lightly. Or, indeed, prospective students, their families and school head teachers accepting without complaint what they might see as a 'loss' of 'their' places at elite institutions, in order to satisfy government ideas about widening access.

For many other institutions, however, the market conditions of student demand will not permit the 'luxury' of selecting students, so they must recruit by marketing themselves and managing their admissions requirements accordingly. In both cases 'reputation' and appeal to particular social communities, and their ideas about the purpose of higher education, may be a key deciding factor in student decisions to apply.

In strategic terms I think there can be an issue of over-reliance on high entry standards, with managers and academics persuading themselves that a high entry level means a low expenditure of effort on supporting transition, the belief perhaps being that the academically 'bright' entrants will progress with relatively 'light touch' support and teaching. Or, put another way, there may be an assumption that high performance can be expected of students without the need for staff time to be consumed by measures to ensure academic engagement.

This rather overlooks the scale of change involved for individuals coming to university and the opportunity to use first year as a formative academic experience rather than as a simple extension of school-level learning. A high entry-level position and a strong historical position in the job market can dampen down interest in specific measures to develop employability. However, since it is often the case that universities which can apply highly selective conditions of entry are also relatively well placed in the research leagues, one can see why this might be an attractive approach from a staff perspective. By contrast, universities which are firmly in the 'wider access' market may feel the exact opposite, and be prepared to invest substantially in measures to smooth transition, hopefully enabling them to retain a higher proportion of recruits.

The other four elements of the model refine the question of strategic manipulations of factors, to reduce uncertainty and optimize the FYE . The key questions are:

- Will driving up entry requirements and intensifying competition for places be sufficient on their own, and if not what else needs to be done?
- If this strategy is not available in all circumstances any way, what else can be done?

Factor 2: Unified course and career track degree programme

A combination of high entry standards and a degree which is clearly vocational/professional in nature is likely to increase the likelihood of high retention/completion. For example, traditional professions such as law, medicine and pharmacy display these features. This is not to say that everyone who is admitted will complete; however, it is more likely that 'drop-outs' will go via transfer to another course as a result of a change of mind, or as a consequence of individual circumstances.

Factor 3: Strong departmental identity and reputation

Like Factor 2, if combined with the others this factor should enhance retention and success by emphasizing 'membership' of a community, and with that a greater sense of belonging. Identity cannot only be defined in communal academic and professional terms, but can be expressed through the physical environment. Thus a department which has its own building, or part of a building, and clearly defined spaces, will provide a strong sense of place and belonging, particularly if the departmental space encompasses key supports such as library and IT facilities and dedicated social space. Matters of decoration and surroundings can add to this effect.

Reputation can be evidenced in many ways – historical eminence, research ratings, 'star' graduates all combine to give a strong sense to entrants of having 'made it'. It is more likely to be achieved in degree programmes which are unified in their structure, and more likely to be problematic where students are admitted to a broad 'faculty'-type degree, where they may not have a departmental home until after first year.

Where a department can offer some features – high reputation, but not others – dedicated space, the emphasis must be on compensating for that weakness, by putting more effort into other factors.

Factor 4: Specific first-year programme linked to course design and programme of study

It might be thought that, if the previous factors are present and well developed, there is not much need to design a first year experience, leaving the natural coincidence of powerful influences to do their work unaided. This would be naïve, mainly because effective formative transition experiences do not just happen; they require thought, effort and specific measures. For example, a first year course design which links student monitoring with active, engaging teaching, good feedback and transparent assessment is much more likely to get the best out of highly qualified entrants than one which is not so coherent. Equally a well-designed first year will multiply the benefits of reputation and vocational focus, whereas a badly designed first year will undermine them.

It is not surprising, therefore, that so much work by FYE specialists is concentrated on devising, describing and evaluating such programmes.

Factor 5: Dedicated staff and supportive management

This seems to me to be a precondition for good design and student-centred practice. However, it is perhaps the most problematic area, given the lack of status and career development opportunity for colleagues who are willing to give their efforts.

Decision making in practice

If all five factors can be combined in a given context, to channel decisions and resources into the most appropriate set of measures for the institution, it is likely that the FYE would be enhanced in that institution.

However, it is unlikely that these conditions will obtain uniformly across all areas of a university. Clearly, there will be areas where recruitment is difficult, where students are admitted to a faculty, rather than to a degree or department, and where monitoring information will be difficult to obtain quickly. Staff–student ratios may be such that close contact with students is inhibited. There will be areas where, for whatever reasons, student engagement and motivation are restricted and where courses show weaker retention and completion rates.

Nonetheless, the model can be used to target effort based on a reasoned view of which variables are most in need of attention. Deterioration in any area signals a need for action, and effort can be targeted at improving or maintaining each part. Thus retention and progression problems could be minimized, where that is the key issue, by manipulating the factors to that end. Additionally student satisfaction might be increased, both generally and in terms of specific concerns, such as feedback and assessment. Beyond those obvious directions, one is faced with the whole range of strategic planning scenarios, with varying degrees of certainty and ambiguity.

For example, Factor 1 is the most likely to be high on the list of topics every institution must consider in formulating its future plans and strategic emphasis. It may also be the one subject to most environmental change over time. Clearly even the traditionally most sought after institutions now need to respond to pressures for equality of opportunity. All institutions need to look to longer term demographic changes, shifts in the nature of pre-university curriculum and the future of graduate labour markets, even if accurate forecasting is difficult.

However, it is perhaps the many 'middle ranking' institutions where the future may look most blurred, and which have the greatest challenge in matching their recruitment practices to the available pool of entrants and the potential of the labour market to soak up ever more graduates. These are the institutions which will be trying to balance research and teaching missions and to devise suitable staffing and estate strategies to underpin their plans against relatively constrained finances and income streams. Prioritization will be their key dilemma, and their leaders will be acutely aware of the risks in making major changes in their profile of activities.

For example, a strategic shift in the direction of increased research activity, possibly forcing a generally reduced commitment to teaching, could backfire in the future if fewer students enrol and anticipated research success is not forthcoming. Student applications, if lost to a decline in reputation for good teaching and support, are hard to regain quickly. This is a dramatic scenario, to illustrate the risks which may be perceived. It is to be hoped that no institution would make such a shift without considering those risks.

Looking to the position of the 'newer' institutions, I suggest that it is less likely that the next two decades will see a wiping out of 'weaker' institutions due to reduced demand/fiercer competition etc. than that different patterns of higher education will emerge, and become more valued and accepted by society. I anticipate that one consequence of massification may be a pressure to revise our notion of higher education as a fairly immutable league table of institutions, with clearly definable 'top', 'middle' and bottom' rankings. In the future, it may be more plausible to think in terms of 'zones' within higher education, containing quite different kinds of 'universities', serving a variety of needs. The current UK and Australian government reviews of HE may offer some indications of what the future may hold.

Drawing back a little from such crystal ball gazing to more immediate local decisions, the model of decision making based on five key factors can be used as follows.

- Factor 1 is a powerful means to focus thinking not only on the numbers of students admitted to first year but also their nature and degree of preparation for study and engagement. However, it should not on its own be used to determine the FYE strategy or specific measures. The other four factors must be taken into account.
- Factors 2, 3 and 4 should, in combination, form the core of all short- to medium-term strategic action plans, although there will obviously be some difference in approach and emphasis on Factors 2 and 3, depending on different degree structures.
- Factor 4 should receive attention in all circumstances, and in all universities, for this is the factor with most direct impact on the student experience of academic and social engagement. I suggest that at least some of the ideas presented in Chapters 3 and 4 should be considered in that discussion.
- Factor 5 is very closely linked to Factor 4, since it is only through valuing staff commitment over time that good course designs can be delivered and improved. A career structure that values the lecturer's task in supporting student transition will make that work easier, although not without challenges. This would include, for example, the need to maintain dedication, to devise effective teaching and other practices and to evaluate and innovate first year teaching.

Now that we have some ideas about making strategic decisions, let us look at how different kinds of strategy might have evolved over time to define current baseline starting points in your institution, and how they might be changed by applying the decision-making model. This is an important component of the framework, as the baseline conditions provide the immediate context for change-oriented decision making. By linking decision making with an account of the local policy legacies, and a consideration of possible strategies, we can illuminate the strategic moves needed to develop a new level of coherence in developing the FYE.

Institutional FYE strategy types: conceptual tool 2

The investigation of how every institution got to its present position on the FYE is beyond the scope of this book. However, Table 5.2 shows a nascent typology of institutional strategies to analyse/categorize institutions, the better to channel future development. In practice colleagues can use this as a way of getting a perspective on where their university might sit on FYE strategy, how it got there and where it might go next. These questions can be informed by the outcome of the sort of strategic decision options arising from the decision-making model.

Table 5.2   Typology of institutional strategies for the FYE

Institutional strategy	Pros	Cons
1 Status quo: Leave well enough alone and react to 'problems'	Allows focus on specific, defined situations, avoids larger reorganizations, contains troublesome situations	Vulnerable to internal/ external pressures and trends; fails to keep pace with change and increases the difficulty of eventual change
2 Best practice: Make a 'shopping list' of problems, identify 'solutions' developed in other institutions ('best practice'); try to transplant them	Fits the popular 'using best practice' perception of educational development; likely to be championed by staff who are attracted to the new idea	Encourages piecemeal initiatives, can be undermined by difficulties in adapting measures to local circumstances
3 Re-engineering academic practice: Innovate in teaching and assessment practices at course unit/department level	Addresses the pedagogical dimension of FYE and can provide a consistent level of experience to all students in the class	May be driven by individual champions and seen as 'a project' by colleagues; may not survive the innovation period; may not be adopted more widely

4 Whole-course renovation: Implement a course/unit design which aligns student learning to transition needs and lays down foundations for academic and personal progression	Integrates good educational practice with practice at class level, and may influence progressive development of the whole degree course	Requires champions, institutional support, concrete decisions, and sustained staff involvement; may be seen as too 'radical' or 'difficult' by lecturers and academic managers

These might be seen as a simple hierarchy, but it is more complex than it appears. Combined with the outcomes of an analysis of the five decision-making factors, these four broad strategic categories begin to take on the form of potential goals for organizational development of the FYE.

For example, a decision to improve retention and student satisfaction by focusing on course design/dedicated staff, aligned to a desire to re-engineer academic practice, might be distilled as shown in Table 5.3:

Table 5.3 Changing strategic direction of the FYE

Issues	**Decision point**	**Strategic direction**
Improve retention/student satisfaction	Concentrate on specific FY programmes linked to course design and programme of study	From: status quo To: re-engineering academic practice Innovate in teaching and assessment practices at course unit/department level

How this might have come about will depend on local circumstances and the outcomes of some process of strategic decision making or strategic 'moves', as I will describe them below. However, before considering this process, I shall introduce the ideas of 'risky shifts' and 'rate-fixing' as key conditions of change.

Rate fixing and risky shifts: conceptual tool 3

I introduce the idea of risky shift/rate fixing to give a very practical handle on the matter of institutional change. Before making a commitment, leaders and their colleagues will want to estimate the scale of change proposed in terms of the risk involved, and the degree of staff change required in particular. These are not simple matters of quantification and direction. Making any kind of shift is as much a matter of perception as anything else, hence the importance of looking at change in the FYE through the decision-making and strategic lenses detailed above, to remove some of the distractions represented by a lack of clarity in focal awareness. Equally, any proposal to change the job content and priorities of staff, to change the 'rate' as it were, is likely to engender powerful forces of suspicion and resistance, which need to be brought out and managed openly.

Risky shift

In essence, the notion of risky shift acknowledges that institutional leaders, and other stakeholders, will tend towards caution when faced with proposals which imply a move from the status quo, unless the status quo has become untenable. For example, a proposal to move from a familiar central service model of provision to a whole-course renewal process of adopting transition pedagogy might well be seen as a significant risk by many of the stakeholders. Consequently, however well argued and evidenced the proposal might be, it would still be resisted.

This has tended to be the dilemma for educational developers seeking large-scale pedagogical change, and I discussed the issues in some detail in Chapter 3. In that discussion I favoured the notion of changing the incentive structure for academic staff. The following discussion of rate fixing may be seen as a necessary aspect of making incentives realistic and effective in terms of changing work practices.

Rate fixing, academic staff and strategic change

Every formal structure involving teaching staff represents a situation where the 'rate' for teaching activity and effort will have been preset in the form of a particular combination of teaching methods, allocation of time etc. This rate will have evolved over years, influenced by disciplinary and departmental norms, and become embedded in the way a given department conducts its teaching. Whilst this rate may not be written down in a formal 'contract' or sets of 'instructions', it will be a powerful influence on how lecturers, particularly new lecturers, behave. It may be 'refixed' by the voluntary acts of lecturers who want, for various reasons, to teach differently and thereby reconstitute the combination of teaching methods. However, there may well not be a particular requirement on colleagues to embrace the new 'rate' if they choose not to, or to adopt its particulars to the same extent as the more engaged colleagues. Witness the sharp differences in adoption of various digital technologies within the same university, indeed within the same department.

Thus on entering a department a new lecturer may find that the rate for teaching generally, and first year teaching in particular, is already 'fixed' in terms of acceptable effort/time spent/methods used etc. This rate can be enforced by subtle, collegiate pressures to conform to what may be presented as disciplinary/departmental norms, and which may be related to powerful influences such as probationary requirements and future career progression. For example, if the local 'rate' for teaching is presented as being the most suitable to allow components of the research 'rate' e.g finishing PhD, being included in the Research Assessment Exercise (RAE), presenting at key conferences, getting on a funding bid etc., it will prove difficult to resist. The headline message becomes: if you teach this way, that will be sufficient for probation, and will ensure that you have more time and energy for the research activity you need to get promoted.

Institutions may formally deny this scenario, pointing to the importance they attach to teaching in their mission statements and alluding to its importance for probation and promotion. However, HoDs and senior research managers may have much more power to influence the situation of academics, and in faculties with research missions and a need to compete effectively for scarce research funds it is easy to understand why they might exert very considerable pressure to counter any tendency to take teaching 'too seriously'.

Equally, the institution's admission position as a student selection or student recruitment university can have a bearing on the situation, since it may well be argued that the high quality of students selected argues for a 'light touch' approach to teaching, and therefore no need to re-engineer academic practice. A combination of *status quo* and *best practice* measures may be seen as sufficient in that admission scenario. Equally, departments in that university which have difficulty selecting suitable entrants, and have to recruit students, perhaps from more diverse and less well prepared backgrounds, may find themselves squeezed by the pressures of having to deploy increased time and effort to teaching, in order to overcome the perceived 'deficits' in their cohorts.

This set of circumstances in a university could combine to define different 'rates' for teaching between departments, and this might result in lecturers, squeezed by pressures to spend more time on teaching and perhaps less on research, in a university which may be strongly asserting a research-intensive institutional strategy. How these pressures can be reconciled is a key strategic question that must be faced by lecturers and institutional leaders, and the outcome will impact the quality of student experience in first year.

Course design, teaching practice and rate fixing

We can elaborate the scenario description by turning to the kind of accounts of university teaching discussed in preceding chapters. Employing a discourse of pedagogical categories, language and literature is a common approach to describing academics' pedagogical approaches to their teaching role and thereby describing the 'job'. This is particularly the case in staff and educational development departments, typically backed by national bodies such as the HEA/ALTC, and in some cases distilled into institutional policy statements on teaching. This is the dominant narrative in discussing what lecturers do about student learning and how they go about it, represented in the many institutional PGCE courses for university teachers accredited by the HEA. To some extent the story can be unfolded rather dramatically as a transformative challenge to established teaching norms and their 'overthrow' by the new ideas. When this rhetorical strategy is employed, it is often met by deep scepticism and criticism from the unconvinced.

In any case, by personifying individuals through the images of the 'transmissive' teacher and the 'constructivist' teacher, we can gain some broad idea of what the different 'rates' or conditions of teaching might look like. Thus the transmissive teacher might constitute the 'rate' for teaching in terms of content coverage, numbers of lectures delivered and exams conducted. The constructivist teacher, by contrast, might define the 'rate' in terms of membership of a team of committed colleagues, managing student group projects, and investing time in detailed feedback etc.

Leaving aside the various arguments over the theoretical soundness of either position, I suggest that the plainer language of employment relations can help refocus thinking. Hence the notion of 'rate for the job' to encompass not simply pay and conditions, but the actual process of work and the 'tools' and 'methods' utilized, allied to the attitudes and values of the people concerned. This may be anathema to some; however, I suggest it is a useful channel of thinking, since it begins to illuminate the powerful determinants of lecturer behaviour, and the limits to change in teaching activity.

Consider the scale of the task in bringing about a change such as that represented by a strategy of *re-engineering academic practice*, in a given department. The change in the rate of the lecturer's job required to secure this strategy may well appear to the people involved to be quite at odds with their current work priorities and perceived career benefits, however attractive the strategy may appear as a way of implementing a constructivist pedagogy. Even in situations where strategic change is required to address an acknowledged threat to the department, such as poor retention or significant student dissatisfaction, the potential for resistance is considerable where teaching, particularly first year teaching, has historically been undervalued.

This is not to suggest that university lecturers can be easily divided into Luddites or revolutionaries. However, I do maintain that significant course redesign can be usefully considered as an exercise in 'resetting the rate' of actual activity. This is an aspect of our thinking which has been rather overshadowed by the edifice of pedagogical theory and literature.

A model of institutional dynamics: conceptual tool 4

The FYE is a complex phenomenon, where the strands of pedagogical theory and practice, institutional strategy, policy and human resource

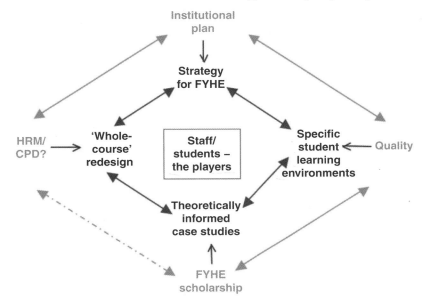

Figure 5.2 Change forces

management intersect, or, more often than not, do not. The forces for positive change entailed in each strand can easily become forces of confusion or conflict. In Figure 5.2 I try to display some of the most influential forces in relation to each other. My purpose is to identify potential solid linkages, and one key area where connectivity is very weak.

It should be plain in modern universities that a level of organizational professionalism is required because of the sheer scale of operations and the demands of external accountability. The institutional plan therefore appears at the top of the figure, to indicate the assumed power of a rational, evidence-based and forward-looking tool to guide activity, priority and human resource management (HRM). In the outer diamond, the plan can be equally strongly linked to quality assurance and enhancement, with connections to FYE scholarship, whilst on the inner diamond the institutional plan is shown directly linked to an FYE strategy plan. I believe this is exactly what has happened over time as strategic problem areas like retention and student satisfaction have become pressing matters of institutional business. In that situation, the FYE is seen as a response to the problem, and links in the FYE scholarship as a source of effective approaches and efficient measures to impact the learning environment, thereby mitigating issues of disengagement or drop-out. This dawning of awareness might be characterized as the beginnings of a move towards the university making a risky shift in its approach to core matters of teaching, learning, course design and so forth.

Looking at the inner diamond, it is possible to see powerful, direct links being forged between scholarly ideas, particularly expressed in terms of the kind of case studies described in Chapters 3 and 4. Thus a whole-course strategy is perfectly possible if all of the links are direct and consciously articulated to that end.

However, I have identified the weak link in the chain as the connection between the scholarship, with its solid connections to other parts of the institutional dynamic, and the institution's crucial human resource and continuing professional development (CPD) domain. Unless the link can be drawn as firmly as the others, then well-intentioned strategic plans and local attempts at innovation will be undermined by lack of a critical mass of understanding and commitment on the part of the academic staff. At this point my notion of rate fixing may provide some insights and directions for change.

This graphic is quite open-ended in that different institutions will offer different profiles of relationship and dynamic from the one I have outlined. However I believe that it does identify the main forces for change in the institutional approach to managing and enhancing the FYE.

Having explored some potential strategic tools which might help clarify the FYE as a strategic issue, I should like to extend the discussion by considering some practical moves which might be taken in order to bring about change.

Key moves in developing a first year strategy (a worked example of the strategy process – from retention to success)

The preceding sections of the framework have illuminated FYE strategy analytically and in terms of human resource issues and institutional willingness to change. It is now time to look at strategic planning in the round, and to try and condense what can be a messy process of committees, working parties, reports and inevitable distractions into a template which can be used to plan and organize strategic development into a tighter time frame.

The moves: stages in reconceptualizing the FYE

That template is described by three distinct but mutually supportive 'moves' in strategy development, piloting, implementing and evaluation.

- Move 1: Acknowledge the FYE and transition as strategic operations combining pedagogical and business activities. This may be initiated and driven by concerns with retention, wider access, employability, or other contingent pressures. A cross-institutional group may be the best way to investigate current situations and suggest change.

- Move 2: Work through a plan of research/consultation with stakeholders to identify the main features of the local FYE and to raise awareness. This informs the decision-making process and helps to formulate policy and set objectives for development within the main institutional plan.
- Move 3: Implement changes at course level and link up all aspects of the FYE to the normal process of annual academic reporting from departments, so that FYE-specific measures can be tracked across the university and checked for consistency and effectiveness over time.

I advocate time limiting the moves in order to maximize control over these critical processes, and to avoid dissipation of effort due to other organizational pressures. For example:

- Move 1/2 contained within no more than two academic years. In doing so you may have to challenge the overlap between decision-making time frames and the academic year cycle and bring them into closer alignment.
- Move 3 managed by a transition phase of up to two academic years.

I believe that time limiting increases the likelihood that the FYE project will result in action on improvement, and reduces the danger of it drifting into paper exercises, or a set of partial, unconnected changes.

The staging of the three moves can be iterated by pilot projects which overlap the phases and inform each other, rather like a spiral of development. There may also be multiple tracks to take account of different baseline conditions, for example some areas of the university may be well advanced at the outset and may be viewed as potential 'good practice' exemplars. However, it is unwise to over-rely on the 'best practice' rubric, as measures may not be readily transferable. Better to refer to some principles of good educational practice and devise first year 'packages' which 'best fit' local circumstances.

Table 5.4 links sections one and two of the framework.

Table 5.4 The four conceptual tools and the process of strategic development

Reconceptualizing FYE	Strategy development process
1 Decision making model: allows key variables to be manipulated to fit circumstances and priorities	Move 1: establish a small working group to: gather information and stakeholder views; survey student experiences of FYE; meet all academic HoDs; meet senior officers and student union representatives. Prepare an initial action plan identifying main actions and responsibilities

2 Typology of institutional strategies: allows broad choice of approach and channelling of decisions	Move 1/2: identify the nature of the local 'status quo' and the underpinning factors; consider broad change options. Raise awareness and build support. Begin to consider the risks and rate fixes involved
3 Risky shift and rate fixing: identifies key structural and human resource challenges to be met in implementing strategic decisions	Move 2: initiate cycles of change in culture and activity. Consider likely stakeholder responses to innovations in teaching and associated systemic changes
4 Model of institutional dynamics: connects key aspects and shows relationships between different organizational levels and functions	Move 2/3: use the developmental heuristic for conducting in-depth strategic analysis of pilots; reorganization of staff development, institutional management information systems, provision of strategic seminars

Key reconceptualization and strategic directions to draw down from this work that align with our best understandings of the FYE would be likely to include:

- shifting policy emphasis *from* student retention *to* student success, so that the university is organized around achieving very high completion rates through targeted efforts on retention whilst enhancing student engagement and performance;
- overcoming fear of the 'risky shift' and finding ways to facilitate the 'rate refixing' required to introduce significant new academic practices;
- bringing about a significant and sustained uplift in the amount of attention, priority and resources applied to the FYE;
- identifying a suitable locus for senior management direction of the university's FYE organization.

The outcome of these moves should be a new improved FYE 'package' for students, which has the commitment of staff and tangible support from management.

A key issue is accessing student views of the FYE and suggestions to improve the experience. The following notes suggest two practical approaches – the *questionnaire survey* and the combined *pyramid review and focus group*. A third *individual trace* approach is also described. These approaches are perhaps most relevant to Moves 1 and 2, but they can be incorporated into ongoing student feedback mechanisms and maybe as complements to national surveys such as NSS.

The student voice – a major component of Moves 1 and 2

Questionnaire surveys might be best conducted at faculty/department levels, but lecturers may find the suggested questions worth considering in terms of their classes in any case. The pyramid review approach can be carried out at class level, although you may want to involve an 'outsider' (for example an educational developer?) to conduct the session and write up a report.

Student questionnaires

Devising a survey instrument should be possible in-house, drawing on the expertise of academic staff, and online implementation within the scope of any university with a VLE. Initial returns should be presented to relevant committees and made widely available for information and comment. If done in stages, i.e. spread over first year, the initial response can identify questions which should be cross-tabulated, and also identify focal themes for later stages of the survey. The benefits of a local survey would include:

- deeper and more nuanced information than national surveys;
- engaging staff/students locally, at course and department levels.

The following questions provide lecturers with a basic template for a systematic survey of the views of first-year students.

Broad questions you may want to address by a survey

These are the main questions you could hope to be illuminated by data from the survey. Decide on priority areas where data will help channel effort on identified changes.

- What do first years expect from university?
- Is the faculty/department/course living up to the expectations?
- Do student experiences vary?
- Are variations related to a particular sub-group factor e.g. age, gender?
- How well do they settle in?
- Do they orient round the 'lowest common denominator' of academic achievement?
- Is paid employment a significant matter?
- Has the faculty/department/course responded to increased numbers/ more varied backgrounds?

For example: three or four broad areas of investigation during a first year.

Area 1: Expectations, experiences, realities (main focus for first semester)

These factors are seen as very influential in determining initial and subsequent attitudes, behaviour and outcomes. Specific questions to ask students:

- How well informed were you about what to expect?
- Did schoolteachers have the information you needed?
- Did you have enough information about courses to make a satisfactory choice?
- Did you have information about teaching at university?
- Did you have information about the standards required?
- Was finance an issue in deciding to come to university?
- Were career prospects an issue in deciding to come to university?
- Was the Open Day useful?
- Was the pre-registration process effective?
- Did faculty orientation in freshers' week help clarify expectations?
- Did department orientation help?
- Did lecturers give helpful advice about course choice?
- Is teaching at university different from school?
- Do you find it easy to approach staff for help?
- Did lecturers spend time explaining assessment practices?
- Have you read the university marking scheme?
- Did university courses build on school subjects?
- Was final year at school a good preparation for university?
- What was your assessment feedback like?
- Did you perform as well as you expected?
- Did you put in as much effort as you could have?
- Do you like the campus environment?
- Do you know where to get help and support?

Area 2: Time commitments (main focus for early semester 2; may need an additional diary exercise to obtain accurate data)

This area is important in giving a context by identifying how much time students are putting into classes and learning activities and how they are balancing competing commitments. There is also interest in estimating how engaged they are with the university learning community in terms of having a presence on the campus and being in touch with others.

- How many days a week do you come to the university?
- How many hours do you spend attending classes?
- How long do you spend on private study?
- Do you contribute to online discussions?
- Do you discuss classes with other students?
- Do you share notes with other students?

- How regularly do you email other students?
- How regularly do you email lecturers?
- How often do you visit class websites?
- Have you joined any clubs or societies?
- How many hours a week of paid employment do you do?
- Do you find it hard to meet all your commitments?

Area 3: Intellectual challenge (spread over both semesters)

This is an important area for motivation and application to study, and should also help explore student views of the relevance of courses.

- Do your subjects keep your interest?
- Are your subjects intellectually challenging?
- Do you go beyond the lecture notes for information?
- Are you mainly interested in getting a basic pass?
- Do you take part in classroom discussions?
- Do you prepare for tutorials by reading recommended texts?
- Do you skip classes?
- Do you skip classes if notes are on the web?

Identifying sub-groups within the population:

- Age (school leaver etc.)
- Gender
- Home/hall residence
- Nationality
- Paid employment status

It would also be helpful to be able to correlate actual achievement against expectations, perceptions, commitments etc. It is important to check for correlation between entry-level profile and first year marks.

Pyramid discussion: 'First year experience: expectations and experiences'

This method was used by the author in 2006/07 for a Scottish QAA-sponsored project in Scotland. The following notes detail the outline for the three interrelated approaches to obtaining student views and insights from face-to-face methods, as an alternative or complement to a questionnaire. This method can be used with whole-class groups, and with groups across departments or year of study.

Basics

The pyramid discussion elicits three levels of response: individual, small group, whole group. Individual/group response is distilled on pro-formas, and the whole-group discussion is conducted as a plenary, with contributions noted. This mitigates group discussion effects by ensuring that each individual submits personal views in writing. Analysis is based on and mirrors the flow of discussion, using the pro-formas and plenary notes. A report is produced and circulated as a draft to all participants for comment and clarification.

A4 pro-forma(s)

Questions:

- What influenced your decision to apply to university?
- What keeps you going?
- What are the differences between your expectations and the experience?
- Specify at least three things which would improve the student experience and try to identify who you think should make the improvements. You can include yourself/other students.

The following sample list of relevant factors against each question is for facilitators to use on the day, and subsequently to support analysis of the session:

What influenced you to apply to university?

- School, family, friends
- School as preparation/advice and guidance
- Perceived job prospects, specific career
- Intrinsic interest in subject/study
- Attracted by the lifestyle
- Nothing else to do
- Other

What keeps you going?

- The teaching, the lecturers, intellectual challenge
- Friends and social life
- Ambition
- The place, the atmosphere
- What you do with your time
- Other

What are the differences between your expectations and the experience?

- Does university build on school subjects?
- Are workload, demands, standards, assessment what you expected?
- Have study patterns changed?
- Is the social life OK?
- Other?

Some of the main research areas probed by the pyramid discussion:

- Expectations – met/unmet; degree of difference/likeness
- Experiences – positive/negative; critical incidents
- Academic/social/employment dimensions – balance; challenges; problems
- Suggestions for change

Focus groups

You may need to devise a concrete and open-ended scenario to introduce the discussion. This may require local knowledge about your institution, but should be general enough to reflect common experiences. For a pilot focus group, you can say that the point of the discussion is:

- to explore student interpretations of key terms e.g. engagement/empowerment;
- to get views on what might enable greater engagement/empowerment.

In the meantime, some *key word* and question probes:

Engagement

- What sort of *prior information* did you have about university? Was it useful?
- What sort of *aspirations* do you have for university?
- Are school/university *academic standards* different?
- Is university easier/harder than school?
- Have you had any *assessments* yet? What was that like?
- Do you have to *attend* every day? Do you have much free time for study? *What do you do* in practice?

Empowerment

- Do you get help to *achieve* your potential?
- What sort of *help* do you get/what else would you like?
- How did you make your *course choices*?

- Did you have much free choice?
- Do you find *other students* supportive?
- Do you get asked for *your opinion* about your course etc?
- Do you feel you are listened to?

The two areas may overlap, so you will need to be flexible in managing the discussion, as it may not be easy to do it in two halves.

Individual trace

The target is to get a least 20 people to keep a diary/write a reflection on their first year, and then spend about an hour being interviewed. If you achieve that target you will have significant in-depth data which can be analysed for variation as much as consensus.

Diary/reflection format

This needs some discussion/negotiation and consultation within your institution regarding any local equivalents.

The interview

Interviewers start by indicating that they are interested in the interviewee's personal perceptions of first year, expressed in his or her own words. Interviewers should concentrate on keeping focus on their interviewee's views, and not get drawn into giving their own opinions, or indications of what they think is relevant/important. This takes skill and may benefit from practice. You should tape record and transcribe the interviews.

Analysis

This can be done in two stages:

1 Application of software like AtlasTI or NuDIST to transcripts using open codes. This will produce a general analysis of what the pool of interviewees talked about, and can be presented using both quotes for items and bar/pie charts of the pattern of responses.
2 In-depth analysis of the main factors of variation in the pool which can be represented as a shortlist of key factors, which can be said to display the main variations in perception of the first year. (There is little evidence that this form of qualitative analysis has been applied to researching student views of the first year.)

A distillation of key principles

This final section of the chapter offeres a generic account of strategic points about the FYE, presented in a form which academic managers and administrators may find useful as a guide to developing local policy statements. The section comprises key guiding principles for practice, a specimen statement of institutional aims and a checklist of good practice. The critical management issue for an institution is to devise ways of implementing an FYE which offers students support and a challenging education throughout first year that equips them for success. The primary initial challenges are likely to include:

- refining current practices and introducing new approaches;
- improving efficiency and effectiveness;
- developing equal levels of commitment across the university;
- building capacity and commitment for transformational change.

Key principles for practice

Development may be focused initially on issues like improving retention and student satisfaction, but, whatever the catalyst, I suggest that institutions should ground their FYE development in several key principles:

- Improvement does not happen by chance
- A legacy of dispersed activity is insufficient
- Simply adding on 'special' programmes is inadequate
- A strategic approach informed by institutional research is essential
- Change will take time, resources and sustained effort

Five institutional aims for FYE and transition

1 A comprehensive, systematic approach to transition, which is appropriate to the kind of university you are in, student-centred and consistent with national/international understanding of good practice.
2 To impact on all first year students, and direct entry students in their first year of attendance, with specific provisions for special populations and appropriate follow-up into second and subsequent years.
3 To involve a wide range of student/staff engagements as part of a 'first year community' who are committed to entailing good transition experiences in their daily activity and who are valued for their commitment.
4 The evaluation and enhancement of activities and initiatives as a regular part of the university's annual and longer term planning and improvement cycles.

5 The need to prioritize action at university level to ensure appropriate value, resources and sustainability over time.

Key objectives will be to achieve efficiency and effectiveness gains and to build capacity for transformational change in subsequent years.

A checklist: four dimensions of good practice

The university will ensure revision and improvement of the student experience by combining at least four interrelated dimensions. These are:

Explicitness and visibility

Leadership and designated responsibility must be clear, effective and accountable, to ensure the following:

- Information about transition issues emphasized in recruitment, enrolment, orientation and throughout induction
- Specific and interrelated activities and systems, particularly within courses of study, which are documented, and embedded in planning and decision-making cycles
- High staff awareness of changes in the composition of first year cohorts and of the specific transitions their students make
- Dedicated staff time, dialogue and debate leading to new initiatives and improvements in the experience students have of first year
- Advice and guidance aimed at improving students' study strategies, skills and motivation
- Proactive identification and support for at-risk students
- Efficient/effective use of central support services
- Preparation and sharing of statements of aspiration and examples of good practice
- Emphasis on and support for co-curricular and social opportunities
- Student involvement in the development of the framework through the gathering and analysis of feedback on their experiences
- Formal procedures for administration, support and monitoring of all of these factors

Engagement and activity

The key task is to challenge at the start any tendency students might have to adopt 'lowest common denominator' behaviour. That is, to challenge minimalist working practices, cynicism, apathy and inertia. The challenge can be made tangible by demanding high levels of attendance, punctuality, contribution and meeting of deadlines from the outset. Other desired qualities to be nurtured over time include: self-awareness, energy, excellence, high performance and success.

Student engagement in the first year experience can be focused by the extent to which students are:

- accepting a set of public ground rules for being a successful, efficient and effective student;
- developing a sense of belonging;
- appreciating academic values, expectations, rigour and practices;
- interacting positively with peers, both academically and socially;
- being known by one or more members of staff;
- balancing effectively all aspects of student life; and
- showing a disposition and motivation to succeed.

In short, it is the difference between students contemplating dropping out and actively pursuing success.

Evaluation and change

There should be a systematic cycle of evaluation at all levels to ensure that we are meeting changing student abilities, expectations and needs, efficiently, effectively and realistically. This evaluation cycle needs to be incorporated in departmental, faculty and university planning processes. Evaluation should be supported by the collection and use of data on: student learning, progress, satisfaction, discontinuation, conversion to second year and other relevant factors. It should be linked to the internal sharing and benchmarking of good practice, and disseminated through reports, annual first year symposia and regular showcasing events. Evaluation should lead to better utilization of existing resources, and acquisition of new resources, to maintain and improve the first year.

Transformation of the learning environment

The target is to agree and implement any major transformations to a time scale that will allow information to be included in the prospectus.

The key areas for consideration include:

1 **Academic timetable**: shape of the academic day, week, semester; realistic appreciation of non-academic calls on student time.
2 **Balance and consistency in the curriculum**: degree of student independence, choice and development of relevant skills; proportion of individual/group and team activity; balance of emphasis on analytical, practical and creative thinking; relationship between disciplinary coherence and interdisciplinary synergy within and across faculties.
3 **Implications for teaching, learning, assessment, course evaluation, educational development, professional development and reward of staff,**

student support services and campus development. For example: addressing the challenges posed by large classes; managing differences between school/college and university expectations and norms for teaching, learning and assessment; use of learning technologies to support first year learning, teaching and assessment; recognizing that students can make inappropriate course choices and facilitating transfer between courses/departments/faculties.

Conclusions

Whilst formal initiatives like transition programmes are a practical institutional response to student engagement, retention, progression and empowerment, it is very important to guard against any tendency to reduce the 'first year experience' to an undifferentiated, uniform set of messages and events, exclusively about academic considerations, or formal university agendas. Students are likely to experience 'multiple first years' as they move from one context to another and bring their different backgrounds to bear. Equally, given the role of paid employment and changes in student lifestyle, the university is likely to become a less central 'place' for students than it was in the past. There is also a balance to be struck, over time and across contexts, between facilitating social engagement and academic engagement.

These factors may offer an agenda for complementary approaches to transition. Diversity, heterogeneity, negotiation, empathy and creativity are at least as important values as formality, efficiency, effectiveness and professionalism in efforts to encourage engagement and secure retention.

6

Universities in a changing world: grand narratives and modest proposals

Introduction

If universities are to maintain their reputation for adaptability into the twenty-first century, their leaders will need to manage two key tasks. First, to develop academic strategies which anticipate near futures. Secondly, to concentrate resources and effort on core elements of activity, so as to move them forward in ways that are relevant to the cultural, social and economic conditions of the times. Thus university leaders will need to be reasoned managers and adventurous educators. In both cases the curriculum is a core strategic issue which must be clearly articulated and highly valued as a cornerstone of the university's contribution to education and society.

Curriculum and the FYE in mass higher education

A holistic view of curriculum, which embraces content, pedagogy, process, diversity and varied connections to the wider social and economic agendas, is most likely to offer a rallying point for the various stakeholders in a university. A 'good' curriculum engenders those forms of intellectual development wherein an individual explores a subject domain, and by sharing her or his findings with companions discovers knowledge. Renewing curriculum in the face of changing circumstances is perhaps the key academic task of educators, and provides the superstructure of our daily lives as teachers within and beyond the classroom.

Subject domains may be represented in terms of academic disciplines, and investigated through the flows of disciplinary information and debate channelled by books, seminars, scientific experiment, practical projects and, very often, the internet. Realistic investigation leads, inevitably, to questions of the wise and ethical use of knowledge and information in society. Answering these questions helps define the nature of graduates and their preparedness to take responsibility for work, citizenship and social life generally in the future. Therefore the 'material' of curriculum inquiry encompasses these explorations, and relates them to both their immediate pedagogical circumstances and their wider academic and social connections.

Within the curriculum domain, the FYE is coming to be acknowledged as a powerful focus for academic strategy, primarily for universities, but with increasing recognition of the need to engage first year at university in relation to other forms of education. This particularly refers to pre-entry but also to future employment. In that later aspect lie interesting research questions concerning the nature of relations between work and learning as issues in curriculum development, which can implicate the FYE in their resolution. Formulating and answering such questions would, I contend, take us beyond the basics of 'embedding' key skills and graduate attributes in particular courses, which has been a powerful influence in recent decades. In addition there is very great scope to debate the relationship between higher education, degree-level study and citizenship in the early twenty-first century, again as issues in curriculum development.

The FYE may therefore be conceived as a gateway to the experience of a given curriculum, and also as a major milestone, or crossroad, in an individual's long life of learning. A well-developed FYE can positively influence student success and support innovation in disciplinary teaching and personal development. Universities which have put effort into uplifting the status of FYE activity at all levels are much more likely to be well placed to meet the challenges of the twenty-first century than those which have not.

The continued massification of enrolments will provide an ongoing challenge. However, the consequential growth of a graduate population of unprecedented numbers will be another. The people concerned are coming to represent a critical mass of informed citizens in many nations, and their actions will influence the nature and future direction of economic growth, social responsibility and cultural engagements. How will these generations of graduates come to imagine themselves in the world? Will they be content to trade their degrees and skills in the global marketplace, or will they have additional, even alternative, perspectives? If so, what might they be? How will they view the world after the credit crisis, and what will they do about it? How will they view higher education and what demands will they make on universities? These are key strategic issues just now coming on the horizon for higher education.

Near future society will therefore be characterized in terms of university education experienced in ways which go beyond the old 'elite' models, or even the more recent 'wider access' representation. It is not clear what pedagogical forms this will take, but we must take action to anticipate the change and create those new forms in line with the best of traditional values and contemporary ideas. I suggest that the *lifelong learning* construct offers a suitable entry point for consideration. Information technology transformed late twentieth century economy and society, and I believe the transformation will become more comprehensive as we realize the nature of living in an *information culture*. This observation will provide a second focus for reconsidering the forms of higher education appropriate for the twenty-first century.

In this chapter I will explore some near future influences, which may condition institutional development of curriculum, and the FYE in particular, and suggest some themes that might be pursued. My broad path of argument is to conceptualize the FYE as a field of curriculum inquiry, which can be developed to influence the nature of whole degree courses, thereby shaping the nature of higher education in a given period. Inquiry can be pursued at a number of levels, including the historical and social, as well as the more obvious level of daily practice. A key aim is to suggest powerful connections between the macro world of socio-economic trends, the intermediate world of university strategic management and the micro worlds of student support, teaching, learning and assessment. I believe that making these connections is fundamental to changing and enhancing teaching practice and developing the student experience of first year at university as a significant element of lifelong learning in an information culture.

Hopefully these wide-ranging perspectives on curriculum will offer some new options for near future work on the FYE. However, we should begin by considering the FYE in particular, and the following section will distil key points from earlier chapters to help focus the wider debate.

The five faces of the first year experience

A well-developed theory and practice of the FYE will be an essential strategic tool for consideration of institutional realignments with the changing environment. The condensed account of the FYE given in Table 6.1 is a graphic 'quick fix' on the ideas about the FYE described in this book. Mobilizing that influence involves educational and organizational development, particularly in terms of the incentives needed to motivate staff. This approach is represented in Faces 1–4. Face 5 highlights the significance the FYE has attained for all institutions in relation to boundary influences such as sector leaders, state policy makers and other stakeholders.

Table 6.1 The five faces of the first year experience

Five faces of FYE	Curriculum forms and boundaries
1 Central services provision and efforts of academic 'stalwarts'	The long-standing 'default' position for universities, standing to one side of mainstream teaching. Challenged by massification and the availability of alternative positions

2 Individual lecturers improving their teaching	The academic mainstreaming position described in Chapter 3
3 Curriculum renewal, evaluation and refinement	A movement to align courses constructively in response to transition issues and the pressure for graduate attributes. Outlined in Chapter 4
4 Institutional organization and management	The organizational development required to enhance the FYE. Explored in Chapter 5
5 Sector-wide standards and enhancement	The external dimension of the FYE e.g. national government; HE organizations like HEA, ALTC, QAA

This summary of the FYE takes us up to the present, but that is not the end of the story. Consider this scenario. The FYE is positioned as a focus for the 'last years' of secondary/further education and also the 'first year' of a degree programme, which is itself a component of lifelong learning in a troubled knowledge economy/information society. The FYE is therefore pivotal, and should be treated as such. Is it, as in much past thinking, mainly about equipping newcomers with skills, attitudes and knowledge for higher education study? Or is it really about the early positioning of potential graduates to be lifelong learners in an information-rich twenty-first century? The sensible answer, I think, is both. The next question is how they are to be constructively reconciled. There are three interrelated aspects of higher education and university development which I believe are key to future development:

- The ramifications of the 2008 credit crisis
- Lifelong learning
- Higher education in an information culture

All three will open up new ways of looking at the FYE and perhaps generate new ways of interpreting and applying the ideas detailed in this book.

Credit crisis 2008; recession 2009; recovery 20—?

The current crisis requires some discussion, at least to begin to set an agenda that might be debated over the next five years. It is reasonable to assume that 'constraint' will be the most likely defining influence on universities in that period. However, I would suggest that we cannot simply anticipate 'shrinking' the HE system. We need to plan a future based on larger numbers, unless government completely abandons commitment to wider access and creation of more human capital. Beyond that I would argue that we should take the opportunity to think beyond the familiar OECD human capital model of education and speculate on an enhanced social mission for higher education.

Constraints and questions: 2008–10

When I began writing this book in 2008 the global economic credit crisis was growing with such force that economies round the world were either in recession or anticipating going into recession during 2009. George Soros (2008) has described the crisis in terms of a trend – the expansion of credit and the accumulation of debt – accompanied by a misconception: that markets, if given free reign, would ensure economic well-being. In 2008 the world economy reached a point where the trend and the misconception were no longer sustainable. As a very successful financier and acute economic thinker, Soros is worth listening to. His insights into the irrationality of the supposedly highly rational people at the commanding heights of the global economy are a challenge to all of us who have a stake in reason and the best use of knowledge.

The impact of this crisis on government, business, employment, housing markets and people's confidence for the future was severe. It seems that the thirty-year neoconservative economic orthodoxy which accompanied the massification of higher education, and to an extent shaped its direction, was on the verge of bankruptcy! At time of writing the crisis is still running its course, with daily news reports of further rifts in the financial fabric accompanied by company closures and significant increases in unemployment. It is not clear yet how higher education will be affected in detail, although the *Guardian* newspaper reported on 12 December 2008 that: 'The global economic downturn has wiped at least £250m from the leading British universities' endowment funds' (pp. 1–2).

Important as endowment funds are to the universities which hold them, their dramatic fall in value may be only the tip of the iceberg in terms of university funding overall in the coming period. The same *Guardian* story reported a 'senior' vice chancellor's view that '… the cutback in government spending on universities would be the worst in 25 years'. If this proves to be an accurate prediction, the next few years will be very tough for universities, given that government expenditure cuts and consequent underfunded expansions of numbers have been the paramount constraint factors for decades. Add to this the likelihood that other income streams may be reduced and that many costs will rise, and the future can look very bleak.

Student reactions

What is unclear at this point is the effect of the credit crisis on graduate recruitment over the next few years, and on students' confidence in the value of their years at university, both of which may prove influential on the perceptions of future potential students. Australian and British graduates have been leaving university with significant debt for years, due to government policy on maintenance funding and fees, and students in other nations have similar experiences. Students, and their families, pay towards university, but do so in part because they have been persuaded that it is a sound investment in future earnings. They also accept the likelihood of reduced income due to the years of wage earning deferred in favour of study. There is some evidence that significant numbers of current graduates in the UK are not reaping the immediate salary benefits they may have expected.

It is possible that the impact of economic dislocation on graduate employment will play out in different ways across the sector. Perhaps the graduates of the most prestigious universities, who took 'stronger' courses, will simply continue to succeed, even if first jobs may be harder to obtain. However, what of the students who went to less well established places and took 'weaker' degrees? Will they find their years of work and struggle devalued by recession? Looking beyond the labour market and careers, mortgages are likely to be difficult to obtain without substantial deposits, and graduate salary premiums may not be sufficient to overcome this problem. There is also the amount of debt accumulated during student years to be taken into account. Will these factors also have a differential impact on graduates, depending not only on the prestige and value of their educational 'capital' but perhaps also their family and social backgrounds?

An additional new dilemma for students graduating into the post-credit crisis era will be 'hidden' in the far future of retirement, as graduates have to look to how they will fund their pensions. State pension benefits have always been weak, and now occupational schemes are becoming much less effective, forcing individuals to contemplate dedicating a greater proportion of personal income to provide for their futures. Also, a proportion of their salaries, and the profits of their enterprises, will be going into providing pension benefits for the earlier generations who enjoyed more stable times and better occupational pension schemes. Their parents, perhaps, and retired university lecturers, for example. Consequently it may be that we will begin to see significant intergenerational conflict emerging in the political and social arenas, once the immediate shock of the economic crisis subsides and we can see a clearer picture of its longer term costs.

An economy in recession will inevitably shrink the job markets in many sectors, increase competition for employment and depress salaries. It would be logical for these circumstances to increase the pressures on students to get the most out of their higher education in order to compete successfully in the job market. This in turn will challenge universities, departments and lecturers to enhance their programmes accordingly, or face a backlash of dissatisfaction and possibly a loss of recruits to more attractive competitors.

Institutional responses

These are problems which cannot be solved overnight, and this suggests that universities should act decisively and without delay to review and redesign their courses in order to enhance their undergraduate portfolios. In many cases the educational development work could be substantial – consider the implications of extending some of the examples described in earlier chapters. This will be harder than it might have been in the recent past, given that funds for academic salaries and appointments, for example, are likely to be squeezed very tightly in the short term. It is equally likely that many UK institutions will be 'rewarding' staff for performance in the 2008 Research Assessment Exercise (RAE). Thus, whilst institutions may see enhancing FYE as a strategic objective for the next few years, key academic staff may conclude that the prizes are still going to research.

Higher education: near futures and institutional implications

All of these points and questions from the current economic crisis have substantial potential consequences for the progress of mass higher education. I see at least three big areas arising which demand urgent attention and some in-depth research:

- Are we likely to face serious disillusion with higher education as a consequence of inequalities in the job markets and lower incomes? If so, how might it be expressed?
- How will the 'net generation' cope with recession? In the West at least, they are children of an era which did not experience major economic downturns, and have expectations calibrated accordingly.
- What are the prospects for lifelong learning in hard economic times, and where might higher education fit into the pattern of provision?

These seem to me to be major issues which require substantial research with a combined focus on the education policy agenda, the general social and economic agendas and, crucially, the implications for higher education institutions for at least the next five years. Researchers are likely to face a moving target; however, key areas for institutional strategy will include:

- social, economic and cultural engagement;
- ethos and priorities;
- marketing and recruitment;
- responsiveness to student need;
- redesign of curricula and pedagogical renewal;
- organizational redevelopment.

There may also be new state pressures for change applied to the higher education sector as a whole, and the next few years may be a period of uncertainty and radical changes in sector-wide policy and organization as well as acute pressures on funding.

Opportunities, constraints and questions: 2010–25

What, then, will be the purpose and place of HE in early to mid-twenty-first century? Is it to continue as an education 'factory', turning out the graduates needed to make the 50 per cent participation targets demanded by the new knowledge economy thinkers in governments of the 1990s? Is it to become a network of institutions practising what Rhodes and Slaughter (2006) referred to as 'academic capitalism' in the service of the new economy? Or is it to be a site of critique and hope based on a different vision of the purpose and practice of learning?

In the longer term, the economic crisis may show that the UK and other OECD nations were not the new 'knowledge economies' of recent public policy orthodoxy, but were really debt-ridden, post-industrial societies busily avoiding reality. Those societies now face the consequences of decades of economic imbalances, and credit-driven consumerism, in the form of recession with no clear perspective on the out-turn. The political response is not clear yet, although it is very likely that demands for a radical overhaul of neoconservative public policy will feature in forthcoming elections. This may well be associated with proposals to dramatically raise the profile of environmental issues as key determinants of economic policy and activity.

Disciplinary responses and institutional challenges

One answer may lie with the rapidly growing theme of global environmental crisis in a world affected by energy depletion and climate change. This seems to be a key challenge to science and engineering disciplines in particular. The implications of having to re-engineer transport, construction, energy production and a host of other critical dimensions demand inspiring responses from these disciplines possibly leading to knowledge transfers from the universities, taking form in new enterprises, creating new jobs in a different kind of knowledge economy.

These environmental matters demand responses from the social sciences, the humanities and the business disciplines as well. Other areas which the social disciplines might address include the social and ethical complexity of the early twenty-first century, for example the dynamics of fundamentalism and imperialism and the relationships between the 'war on terror', global inequalities and international economic development. In effect we must begin to define the grand narratives using the academic tools of research, communication and education. The institutional challenge is great and the response will need to be multi-layered, involving:

- renewed purpose and content of HE and institutional reorganization;
- renewed status for teaching and educational development;
- developing institutional leaders who focus on education, society and culture in the broadest sense, and with a wider sectoral perspective than the various current inter-university league tables.

Key pedagogical questions are:

- How will students *engage* educationally with the questions raised by the 2008–10 economic crisis? The answers will, after all, be directly relevant to their development, their careers and personal futures. Will they be satisfied with a curriculum of disciplinary specialisms and 'employability'-related skills, or will they be seeking a broader experience, which is relevant to the issues of the day? If so, what might that renewed curriculum contain and how would it be experienced?
- How should higher education *empower* students to engage academically, and in the wider social sense, with such issues, the better to bring about change? The potential contrast between the narrow 'job'-focused employability of recent years and a wider 'citizen development' perspective is stark, and also very exciting in its potential.

In effect we urgently need to reconsider the place of the university in society, the practice of university education and the role of the student in the university. Answering all of the conundrums of the early twenty-first century is beyond the scope of this book. However, some possible directions can be identified. I contend that we have enough understanding of how to enhance the first year curriculum at least to make a start, which could be a catalyst for systematic renovation of degree programmes.

Higher education, lifelong learning and information culture

The following discussion is grounded in the notion of *lifelong learning* as a way of conceptualizing the university as a key educational node in twenty-first-century society. Allied to this is the view that whatever else happens in our societies in the coming years, the influence of the internet as a key communication channel and source of information will continue to develop and become ever more pervasive.

Lifelong learning and the higher education curriculum in mass higher education

Lifelong learning is an educative process of changes and transformations which shape an individual's ways of being in society. It is most often characterized in the literature through modern notions of formal education related to various social and economic agendas (Candy *et al.*, 1994; Dunne, 1999; Holford *et al.*, 1998; Istance *et al.*, 2002; Scottish Executive, 2003a, b).

Universities should expect to be enriching the overall educational life of the nation. To do this we need to adapt missions and practices to align with the ramifications of population trends and changes in the way people make their living. This will be difficult in times of recession and uncertainty; however, this fact underlines the necessity of thinking beyond the next five years and looking to a wider educational horizon. The connections in Table 6.2 offer some pointers to the broad nature and shape of degree studies conceived of as part of a lifelong learning curriculum.

Table 6.2   Lifelong learning and the higher education curriculum

Lifelong learning themes	Implications for HE curriculum
Greater life expectancy means longer lives of learning	More enrolments and more graduates create a general desire for the kind of knowledge only universities can provide. Barriers between personal and professional identities change to form a need for integrated development. Knowledge for work and knowledge for lifestyle become equally valuable to citizens educated to degree level. Traditional degree structures need to be revised to create appropriate new forms, content and practices
Different and overlapping learning generations in a society defined by periodic vocational change over the life course	As characteristics such as age, gender, vocation and income become more mutable, learning becomes the pervasive social experience channelling change. Universities will not be the only provider of learning, but their unique perspectives on inquiry and research can enrich provision
Learning to learn is decisive in managing life cycles and social change	Self-awareness and the ability to conceptualize new futures, devise change strategies and adapt to new situations come into the foreground. University education can become the key form of adult education in society

Learning and web-based information, communication and community	The web is conceived in constructivist terms in addition to its power to transmit and archive knowledge. Web-based learning grows in sophistication and opens the doors of the university to the public at large
Work and learning coalesce around new forms of work organization and processes characterized by knowledge, information and intellectual work	Notions of graduate attributes and employability continue, but morph into other conceptions and practices as research on the relations between work and learning develops. Transition from university to work will need much greater emphasis in the curriculum
Learning and society become highly integrated as social mobility and diversity demand knowledge-based strategies for engaging citizenship	University knowledge is consciously structured and made accessible as credible knowledge in the public interest to counterbalance bias and prejudice

There is a clear need to devise curricula for lifelong learning to embrace these possibilities. The FYE will be decisive in forming student consciousness as well as skill sets. Whole-course renewal articulated to other learning sectors and situations becomes the major task. This renewal project should become a headline feature of educational development at both sector and institutional levels. I suggest four major questions about lifelong learning in relation to higher education over the next decade:

- Definition and positioning of lifelong learning in state policy?
- Nature and extent of lifelong learning alignments in higher education?
- Impact on learning designs?
- Individual and collective experience of lifelong learning?

Answering these questions would provide a roadmap for curriculum renewal and specific FYE strategies.

Higher education and information culture

We are used to notions of information society and knowledge economy, given their central place in public policy and popular discussion over the last twenty years. We are all well used to a key concept of the information age – the *information explosion* – and many academics bemoan its impact on their capacity to 'keep up' with their disciplines. In more prosaic terms, concern about student misuse, and misunderstanding, of information technology has become ubiquitous under proxy terms like plagiarism. In both arenas the adoption of information technologies and the internet has been widespread and has stimulated pedagogical innovation and course renewal.

However, I believe we have reached a point in time when it is appropriate to take a wider view, and consider ourselves living in an *information culture*. This view is a response to the extent to which *information* as a key social and economic resource has become a fundamental part of our everyday lives and learning experiences. We now experience ourselves accessing, processing, analysing and repurposing information in all our relationships and transactions. This has become the normal state of being in the OECD nations and is a growing reality wherever cheap, easy to use information technology and internet connection is available. Consequently higher education needs to explore the implications of this new situation and devise a way of responding.

What is information culture?

I suggest that the whole of an information culture is greater than the sum of its many parts. I see information culture as a conceptual unity of:

- mobile technology and the internet's capacity to link content and connect people in social and professional networks;
- the varied experiences of digital, multimedia communication by different groups in societies and across cultures;
- the growing tensions between traditional, corporately owned mass media hegemony over what is constituted as 'news' and the capacity of citizens to publish their ideas and opinions to vast 'readerships' via the internet;
- the political debates on freedom of information, surveillance, ownership of and access to state databases;
- the rapidly growing acknowledgement of information and communications systems as core economic components and the need to respond at all levels of education and training;
- the blurring of boundaries between the individual, local, national, international and global spheres of life arising from greatly increased access to information and people;
- the evolution of virtual spaces where people combine to learn, share ideas and develop social action to bring about political change.

These features are coalescing as defining characteristics of the socio-cultural and economic context of twenty-first-century society and should therefore be represented and understood as part of the higher education curriculum.

Universities, the web, lifelong learning and information literacy

Much of the recent impetus behind policy support for lifelong learning has arisen from aspects of the new economy and the reorganization of work subsumed by terms like knowledge worker. Thus higher education has been driven by an agenda of the graduate attributes associated with this phenomenon. What students and employers need in addition is the intellectual, critical ability to act as fully empowered citizens within an information culture, and not simply as employees of a knowledge economy.

This entails universities going some way beyond the incorporation of VLEs, for example, and fixating on problem issues such as:

- information overload and lack of information management skills;
- inappropriate uses such as plagiarism.

I suggest that universities have an opportunity to grasp the high ground of the information culture debate, by making a small imaginative leap, channelling more effort and attention into a project to raise awareness of information culture and embedding suitable response measures in every course design across the curriculum.

The emerging discipline of *information literacy* (Johnston and Webber, 2000, 2003, 2004; Webber and Johnston, 2005) offers a focus for discussion and a guide to possible curricular forms which information literacy might take in higher education. Breivik and Gee (2006) link information literacy to a renewed understanding of the traditional relations between academic libraries and education in a digital world. The relations between information literacy and learning have been the subject of recent work in Australia (Bruce *et al.*, 2006 and Bruce, 2008), which has excited international interest.

Practical work on teaching information literacy can be aligned with the constructivist approach to learning. For example, students would spend more time on tasks designed to encourage deeper processing of information and ideas rather than simply 'finding references' to comply with superficial notions about academic convention. This would take them beyond lecture notes and library shelves to the online information cornucopia, and require them to select, analyse and apply knowledge to complex problems. This in turn would require developing good knowledge of reliable sources, allied with the intellectual ability to formulate and refine search strategies and the searching skills demanded by different databases and web resources. Crucially, information literacy would be an explicit aspect of feedback and assessment strategy.

There are active communities of information literacy researchers, educators and librarians who can be engaged with the FYE, but at present the two communities do not seem to engage closely enough. Changing this would be a useful step in connecting the FYE more closely to notions of information culture, and developing appropriate information literacy in the curriculum. A useful objective would be to begin to connect notions of the FYE to the development of a new engagement between higher education and lifelong learning, through a curriculum which explored and discovered the nature of twenty-first century information culture.

Conclusion

In this book I have tried to make connections between the societal, institutional and pedagogical dimensions of higher education as they relate to the FYE. I have tried to combine pragmatic advice for lecturers in their daily activities with arguments for curriculum renewal and strategic organizational development. If these efforts lead to improvement in the student experience of the first year at university then it will be down to the ingenuity and commitment of colleagues who have adapted some of my notions to fit their situations, and in the process perhaps devise some new approaches of their own.

My final point is one of challenge to all parties with an interest in adapting higher education to the times we live in and the opportunities we can envisage. I believe we have a chance over the next few years to reconnect learning with a wider range of social influences and imperatives than has been common in recent decades. The 2008 credit crisis and ensuing recession have served to expose the frailty of economies focused entirely on endless 'boom'. This project has included the suborning of education to the production of 'human capital', with consequent impacts on the curriculum.

The lessons of 2008 are still being learned, and I am not suggesting that higher education has the responsibility for finding all the answers. However, I hope that one outcome is a renewal of our sense of the holistic mission and obligation of higher education – a mission which may find form in a new curriculum focused on regenerating a 'social capital' of trust and democratic engagement to match the scientific and practical skills of our graduates. Lifelong learning and information culture, in all their diversity, offer at least two practical channels for curriculum development. This seems to me to be a task which needs to start in first year, and develop throughout the whole programme of study.

Appendix

Reports of the Scottish QAA first year enhancement themes

Gordon, G., Project 1 Final Report: The Nature and Purposes of the First Year. www.enhancementthemes.ac.uk/documents/firstyear/ Sector%20Wide%20-%20final%20for%20web.pdf

Johnston, B. and Kochanowska, R., Project 2 Final Report: Student Expectations, Experiences and Reflections on the First Year. www.enhancementthemes.ac.uk/documents/firstyear/StudentExpectations.pdf

Bovill, C., Morss, K. and Bulley, C., Project 3 Final Report: Curriculum Design for the First Year. www.enhancementthemes.ac.uk/documents/firstyear/ Curriculum_Design_final_report.pdf

Nicol, D., Project 4 Final Report: Formative and Diagnostic Assessment and Feedback. www.enhancementthemes.ac.uk/documents/firstyear/ Transforming_assess_fdbk_draft2.pdf

Black, F. and MacKenzie, J., Project 5 Final Report: Peer Support in the First Year. www.enhancementthemes.ac.uk/documents/firstyear/ PeerSupport%20-%20Final%20Draft.pdf

Johnston, B. and Kochanowska, R. (2009) Quality Enhancement Themes: The First Year Experience. Student Expectations, Experiences and Reflections on the First Year. Glasgow: Quality Assurance Agency for Higher Education.

Miller, K., Calder, C., Martin, A., McIntyre, M., Pottinger, I. and Smyth, G., Project 6 Final Report: PDP in the First Year. www.enhancementthemes.ac.uk/documents/firstyear/PDPFinal_Report_2.pdf

Knox, H. and Wyper, J. Project 7 Final Report: Personalisation of the First Year. www.enhancementthemes.ac.uk/documents/firstyear/ Personalisation%20-%20Final.pdf

Alston, F., Gourlay, L., Sutherland, R. and Thomson, K., Project 8 Final Report: Introducing Scholarship Skills. www.enhancementthemes.ac.uk/documents/firstyear/ Scholarship_skills_final_report.pdf

Whittaker, R., Project 9 Final Report: Transition to and during the First Year. www.enhancementthemes.ac.uk/documents/firstyear/Transition%20-%20Final.pdf

References

Anderson, N. and Ostroff, C. (1997) Selection as socialisation, in N. Anderson and P. Herriot, *International Handbook of Selection and Assessment*. Chichester: Wiley.

Andresen, L., Boud, D. and Cohen, R. (2000) Experience-based learning, in G. Foley (ed.) *Understanding Adult Education and Training*, 2nd edn. Sydney: Allen and Unwin.

Angelo, T. and Cross, P. (1990) *Classroom Assessment Techniques*. New York: Jossey-Bass.

Arnold, J. (1997) *Managing Careers in the Twenty-first Century*. London: Paul Chapman Publishing.

Astin, A. (1993) *What Matters in College: Four Critical Years Revisited*. San Francisco, CA: Jossey-Bass.

Australian Government, Department of Education, Science and Training (DEST) (2004) *Development of a Strategy to Support the Universal Recognition and Recording of Employability Skills*. Directions Paper (Report by the Allen Consulting Group). Canberra: DEST.

Baldry, C., Bain, P., Taylor, P. *et al.* (2007) *The Meaning of Work in the New Economy*. Basingstoke: Palgrave Macmillan and Economic and Social Science Research Council (ESRC) Future of Work Programme.

Banks, D.A. (2006) *Audience Response Systems in Higher Education: Applications and Cases*. London: Information Science Publishing.

Barnett, R. and Coate, K. (2005) *Engaging the Curriculum in Higher Education*. London: Open University Press/Society of Research into Higher Education.

Barr, M. J. and Lee Upcraft, M. (1990) *New Futures for Student Affairs*. San Francisco, CA: Jossey-Bass.

Barton, D. (1994) *Literacy: An Introduction to the Ecology of Written Language*. Oxford: Blackwell.

Becher, T. and Trowler, P. R. (2001) *Academic Tribes and Territories: Intellectual Enquiry and the Culture of Disciplines*, 2nd edn. Milton Keynes: Open University Press/Society for Research into Higher Education.

Belton, V., Johnston, B. and Walls, L. (2001) Developing key skills at Strathclyde Business School through the integrative core, in Hockings, C. and Moore, I. (eds) *Innovations in Teaching Business and Management*. SEDA paper 11. Birmingham: SEDA.

Bennett, N., Dunne, E. and Carré, C. (2000) *Skills Development in Higher Education and Employment*. Buckingham: Open University Press/Society for Research into Higher Education.

Biggs, J. (2007) *Teaching for Quality Learning at University*, 3rd edn. London: Open University Press/Society for Research into Higher Education.

Blimling, G. S. and Whitt, E. J. (1999) *Good Practice in Student Affairs: Principles to Foster Student Learning*. San Francisco, CA: Jossey-Bass.

Braxton, J., Hirschy, A. and McClendon, S. (2004) *Understanding and Reducing College Student Departure.* San Francisco, CA: Jossey-Bass.

Braxton, J. M. (2000) *Reworking the Student Departure Puzzle.* Nashville, TN: Vanderbilt University Press).

Breivik, P. and Gee, E. G. (2006) *Higher Education in the Internet Age: Libraries Creating a Strategic Edge.* London: American Council on Education and Praeger.

Brown, G. and Atkins, M. (1988) *Effective Teaching In Higher Education.* London: Methuen.

Bruce, C. (2008) *Informed Learning.* Chicago, IL: Association of College and Research Libraries (A Division of the American Library Association).

Bruce, C., Edwards, S. and Lupton, M. (2006) *Six Frames for Information Literacy Education: A Conceptual Framework for Interpreting the Relationships between Theory and Practice.* www.heacademy.a.uk/italics/vol5–1/pdf/sixframes_final%20_1_pdf

Candy, P. C., Crebert, G. and O'Leary, J. (1994) *Developing Lifelong Learners through Undergraduate Education.* National Board of Employment, Education and Training Report 28. Canberra: Australian Government Publishing Service.

Chickering, A.W. and Gamson, Z. F. (1987) Seven principles for good practice in undergraduate education, *The Wingspread Journal,* 9(2).

Collis, B. and Moonen, J. (2006) The contributing student: learners as co-developers of learning resources for reuse in web environments, in D. Hung and M. S. Khine (eds) *Engaged Learning with Emerging Technologies.* Dordrecht: Springer and Business Media.

Cook, A. E. and Rushton, B. S. (2008) *Student Transition: Practices and Policies to Promote Retention.* SEDA Paper 121. London: Staff and Educational Development Association.

Cook, T. (2003) Roots of attrition, in *Student Retention Conference Presentations, University of Ulster.* www.ulster.acuk/star/resources/resources.htm

Cottrell, S. (2008) *Teaching Study Skills and Supporting Learning.* Basingstoke: Palgrave Macmillan.

Delors, J. *et al.* (1996) *Learning: The Treasure Within. Highlights.* Paris: UNESCO. www.unesco.org/delors/delors_e.pdf

Denholm, J., McLeod, D., Boyes, L. and McCormick, J. (2003) *Higher Education: Higher Ambitions? Graduate Employability in Scotland. A Review of the Issues for the Scottish Higher Education Funding Council and the Scottish University for Industry.* www.shefc.ac.uk/publications/ other/ higher_ education_ambition.pdf)

Drew, S. (1998) *Key Skills in Higher Education: Background and Rationale.* SEDA Special, 6. Birmingham: Staff and Educational Development Association.

DuGay, P. (1996) *Consumption and Identity at Work.* London: Sage Publications.

Dunne, E. (1999) *The Learning Society: International Perspectives on Core Skills in Higher Education.* London: Kogan Page.

Dweck, C. S. (1999) *Self-theories: Their Role in Motivation, Personality and Development.* Philadelphia, PA: Psychology Press.

Edgerton, D. (2008) *The Shock of the Old: Technology and Global History Since 1900.* London: Profile Books.

Edwards, S. (2006) *Panning for Gold: Information Literacy and the Net Lenses Model.* Adelaide, Auslib Press.

Elias, P. and Purcell, K. (2001) *Scotland's Graduates Moving On.* Glasgow: University of Strathclyde and the Industrial Society.

Entwistle, N. and Tomlinson, P. (eds) (2007) *Student Learning and University Teaching*. Monograph Series II: Psychological Aspects of Education – Current Trends. Leicester: British Psychological Society.

Fry, H., Ketteridge, S. and Marshall, S. (2003) *A Handbook for Teaching and Learning in Higher Education: Enhancing Academic Practice*, 2nd edn. London: Kogan Page.

Gabelnick, F. J., MacGregor, R. and Smith, B. L. (eds) (1990) *Learning Communities: Creating Connections among Students, Faculty, and Disciplines*. New Directions for Teaching and Learning. San Francisco, CA: Jossey-Bass.

Gent, I., Johnston, B. and Prosser, P. (1999) Thinking on your feet in undergraduate computer science: a constructivist approach to developing and assessing critical thinking, *Teaching in Higher Education*, 4(4): 511–22.

Gibbs, G. (1992) *Improving the Quality of Student Learning*. Bristol: Technical and Educational Services.

Handy, C. B. (1995) *Beyond Certainty: The Changing World of Organisations*. London: Hutchinson.

Harvey, L. and Drew, S. with Smith, M. (2006) *The First-year Experience: A Review of Literature for the Higher Education Academy*. www.heacademy.ac.uk/assets/York/documents/ourwork/research/literature_reviews/first_year_experience_full_report.pdf

Harvey, L., Moon, S. and Geall, V. (1997) *Graduates' Work: Organisational Change and Students' Attributes*. Birmingham: Centre for Research into Quality, University of Central England.

Hawkridge, D. (2005) *Enhancing Students' Employability: The National Scene in Business, Management and Accountancy*. Prepared for the Higher Education Academy by the Subject Centre for Business, Management and Accountancy. www.business.heacademy.ac.uk/resources/landt/employ/bmaemployability.pdf

Heikkila, A. and Lonka, K. (2006) Studying in higher education: students' approaches to learning, self-regulation and cognitive strategies, *Studies in Higher Education*, 31(1): 99–117.

Henkel, M. (2000) *Academic Identities and Policy Change in Higher Education*. London: Jessica Kingsley.

Higher Education Funding Council for England (2003) *How Much Does Higher Education Enhance the Employability of Graduates?* www.hefce.ac.uk/ pubs/rdreports/2003/rd13_03/default.asp

Hockings, J. and Moore, I. (eds) (2001) *Innovations in Teaching Business and Management*. SEDA Paper 11. Birmingham: SEDA.

Holford, J., Jarvis, P. and Griffin, C. (1998) *International Perspectives on Lifelong Learning*. London: Kogan Page.

Holliday, G. (2005) 'Citizen scoops', *Guardian*, Life supplement, 4 August: 19. www.guardian.co.uk/online/story/0,3605,1541773,00.html

Howe, N. and Strauss, W. (2000) *Millennials Rising: The Next Great Generation*. New York: Vintage.

Howe, N. and Strauss, W. (2003) *Millennials Go to College*. New York: American Association of Collegiate Registrars and Admissions Officers.

Ipsos MORI (2007) Student expectations study: key findings from online research and discussion evenings held in June 2007 for the Joint Information Systems Committee. www.jisc.ac.uk/media/documents/publications/studentexpectations.pdf

Istance, D., Schuetze, H. D. and Schuller, T. (eds) (2002) *International Perspectives on Lifelong Learning: From Recurrent Education to the Knowledge Society.* Buckingham: Open University Press/Society for Research into Higher Education.

Johnston, B. and Kochanowska, R. (2009) *Quality Enhancement Themes: The First Year Experience. Student Expectations, Experiences and Reflections on the First Year.* Glasgow: Quality Assurance Agency for Higher Education. www.enhancementthemes.ac.uk/documents/firstyear/StudentExpectations.pdf

Johnston, B., Van Der Meer, R.B. and Watson, A.C. (2002) Teaching decision making across the curriculum: challenges and dilemmas of integrative studies. Paper presented at the LTSN BEST 2002 Conference: Supporting the Teacher, Challenging the Learner, Edinburgh, 8–10 April.

Johnston, B. and Watson, A. (2004) Participation, reflection and integration for business and lifelong learning: pedagogical challenges of the integrative studies programme at the University of Strathclyde Business School, *Journal of Workplace Learning,* 16:1/2: 53–62.

Johnston, B. and Watson, A. (2006) Employability: approaches to developing student career awareness and reflective practice in undergraduate business studies, in P. Tynjala, J. Valimaa and G. Boulton-Lewis (eds) *Higher Education and Working Life: Collaborations, Confrontations and Challenges.* Amsterdam: Elsevier in association with Earli.

Johnston, B. and Webber, S. (2000) Towards the information literate graduate: rethinking the undergraduate curriculum in business studies, in K. Appleton, C. Macpherson and D. Orr (eds) *Lifelong Learning Conference: Selected Papers from the Inaugural International Lifelong Learning Conference, Yeppoon, Queensland, Australia: 17–19 July 2000.* Rockhampton: Lifelong Learning Conference Committee.

Johnston, B. and Webber, S. (2003) Information literacy in higher education: a review and case study, *Studies in Higher Education,* 28 (3): 335–52.

Johnston, B. and Webber, S. (2004) The role of LIS faculty in the information literate university: taking over the academy? *New Library World,* 105 (1/2) 12–20.

Kember, D. and Kelly, M. (1993) *Improving Teaching Through Action Research.* HERDSA Green Guide No. 14. Campbelltown, NSW: Higher Education Research and Development Society of Australasia.

Kift, S. (2004) Organising first year engagement around learning: formal and informal curriculum intervention. Paper presented to 8th Pacific Rim Conference on the First Year Experience, 14–16 July, Monash University, Melbourne, Australia. www.yhe.qut.edu.au/FYHE_PreviousPapers04/Sally%20Kift_paper.doc

Kift, S. (2005) Transforming the first year experience: a new pedagogy to enable transition. Paper presented to Enhancing Student Success Conference, University of Newcastle, Australia. www.ccc.newcastle.edu.au/student-support/2005conference/Sally%20kift.pdf

Kift, S. (2008) The first year experience in a new higher education landscape: what are the factors influencing the quality of the student experience? What are the priority areas for change and innovation? Paper presented to 11th Pacific Rim First Year in Higher Education Conference 30 June–2 July, Hobart, Tasmania.

Kift, S. and Nelson, K. (2005) *Beyond Curriculum Reform: Embedding the Transition Experience.* Campbelltown, NSW: Higher Education Research and Development Society of Australia. www.edu.au/uploads/documents/Sally%20Kift_paper.doc

King, Z. (2003) New or traditional careers: a study of UK graduates' preferences, *Human Resource Management Journal,* 13(1): 5–25.

Knight, P.T. and Yorke, M. (2003) *Assessment, Learning and Employability*. Maidenhead: Open University Press/Society for Research into Higher Education.

Koch, A. K. (ed.) (2007) *The First-Year Experience in American Higher Education: An Annotated Bibliography*, 4th edn. Monograph 3. Columbia, SC: University of South Carolina, National Resource Center for the First Year Experience. www.sc.edu/fye/publications/monograph/monographs/ms003.html

Kogan, M. (2000) Higher education communities and academic identity, in I. McNay (ed.) *Higher Education and its Communities*. Buckingham: Open University Press.

Krause, K-L. (2005) The changing student experience: who's driving it and where is it going? Paper presented to Student Experience Conference: Good Practice in Practice, Charles Sturt University, Australia. www.cshe.unimelb.edu.au/Krause/StudExpKeynote05.pdf

Krause, K-L. and Coates, H. (2008) Students' engagement in first-year university, *Assessment & Evaluation in Higher Education*, 33(5): 493–505.

Krause, K-L., Hartley, R., James, R. and McInnis, C. (2005) *The First Year Experience in Australian Universities: Findings from a Decade of National Studies*. Canberra: DEST. www.cshe.unimelb.edu.au/APFYP/researh_publications3.html.

Kuh, G. (2003) What we're learning about student engagement from NSSE, *Change*, 35(2): 24–32.

Kuh, G., Cruce, Ty M., Shoup, R. *et al.* (2008) Unmasking the effects of student engagement on first-year college grades and persistence, *The Journal of Higher Education*, 79(5).

Kuh, G. D., Kintzie, J., Schuh, J. H., Whit, E. J. and Associates (2005) *Student Success in College: Creating the Conditions that Matter*. San Francisco, CA: Jossey-Bass.

Kuh, G. D., Schuh, J. H. and Whitt, E. J. (1991) *Involving Colleges: Successful Approaches to Fostering Student Learning and Development Outside the Classroom*. San Francisco, CA: Jossey-Bass.

Land, R., Meyer, J. and Smith, J. (eds) (2008) *Threshold Concepts within the Disciplines*. London: Sense Publishers.

Laurillard, D. (1993) *Rethinking University Teaching: A Framework for the Effective Use of Educational Technology*. London: Routledge.

Lea, M. (2004) Academic literacies: a pedagogy for course design, *Studies in Higher Education*, 29(6): 739–56.

Lea, M. and Street, B. (1997) *Perspectives on Academic Literacies: An Institutional Approach*. Swindon: Economic and Social Research Council.

Lea, M. and Street, B. (1998) Student writing in higher education: an academic literacy's approach, *Studies in Higher Education*, 23(2): 157–72.

Lillis, T. (2001) *Student Writing: Access, Regulation, Desire*. London: Routledge.

Lillis, T. and Turner, J. (2001) Student writing in higher education: contemporary confusion, traditional concerns, *Teaching in Higher Education*, 6(1): 57–68.

Lines, D., McLean, D. and Taylor, R. (2006) Enhancing the curriculum: empathy, engagement, empowerment. Paper presented to Innovations in Student Success, HEA conference, London, 6 February. www.heacademy.ac.uk/resources/archive

Lloyd, A. (2003) Information literacy: meta-competency for the knowledge economy: an exploratory paper, *Journal of Librarianship and Information Science*, 35(20): 87–92.

Lowe, H. and Cook, A. (2003) 'Mind the gap': are students prepared for higher education?, *Journal of Further and Higher Education*, 27(1): 53–76.

Lowis, L. and Castley, A. (2008) Factors affecting student progression and achievement: prediction and intervention. A two year study, *Innovations in Education and Teaching International*, 45(4): 333–43.

Lupton, M. (2004) *The Learning Connection: Information Literacy and the Student Experience*. Adelaide: Auslib Press.

McInnis, C., James, R. and McNaught, C. (1995) *First Year on a Crowded Campus: Diversity in the Initial Experiences of Australian Undergraduates*. A commissioned project of the Committee for the Advancement of University Teaching. Melbourne: Centre for the Study of Higher Education, University of Melbourne.

Manning, K., Kinzie, J. and Schu, J. (2006) *One Size Does Not Fit All*. London: Routledge.

Marton, F., Hounsell, D. and Entwistle, N. (1997) *The Experience of Learning: Implications for Teaching and Studying in Higher Education*, 2nd edn. Edinburgh: Scottish Academic Press.

Mayrhofer, W., Steyrer, J., Strunk, G., Schiffinger, M. and Iellatchitch, A. (2005) Graduates' career aspirations and individual characteristics, *Human Resource Management Journal*, 15(1): 38–56.

Moynagh, M. and Worsley, R. (2005) *Working in the Twenty-first Century*. Leeds: Economic and Social Science Research Council (ESRC) Future of Work Programme/ Kings Lynn: The Tomorrow Project.

National Committee of Enquiry into Higher Education (1997) *Higher Education in the Learning Society* (Dearing Report). London: HMSO.

Nicol, D. J. (1997) *Research on Learning and Higher Education Teaching*. Briefing Paper 45, April. Birmingham: UCoSDA.

Nicol, D. J. and Boyle, J. T. (2003) Peer instruction and class-wide discussion: a comparison of two interaction methods in the wired classroom, *Studies in Higher Education*, 28(4): 473–77.

Nicol, D. J. and Macfarlane-Dick, D.(2004) Rethinking formative assessment in HE: a theoretical model and seven principles of good feedback practice. www.heacademy.ac.uk/ourwork/learning/assessment/senlef/principles

Nicol, D. J. and Macfarlane-Dick, D. (2006) Formative assessment and self-regulated learning: a model and seven principles of good feedback practice, *Studies in Higher Education* 31(2): 199–216.

Nicol, D. J. and Milligan, C. (2006) Rethinking technology-supported assessment in terms of the seven principles of good feedback practice, in C. Bryan and K. Clegg (eds), *Innovative Assessment in Higher Education*. London: Routledge.

Pang, M. F. and Marton, F. (2003) Beyond 'lesson study': comparing two ways of facilitating the grasp of economic concepts, *Instructional Science*, 31(3):175–94.

Pascarella, E. T. and Terenzini, P. T. (1991) *How College Affects Students*. San Francisco, CA: Jossey-Bass.

Pascarella, E. T. and Terenzini, P. T. (2005) *How College Affects Students, Vol. 2: A Third Decade of Research*. San Francisco, CA: Jossey-Bass.

Perry, W. G. (1970) *Forms of Intellectual and Ethical Development in the College Years: A Scheme*. New York: Holt, Rinehart and Winston.

Porter, S. R. and Swing, R.L. (2008) Understanding how first year seminars affect persistence, *Research in Higher Education*, 47(1): 89–109.

Prensky, M. (2001) Digital natives, digital immigrants, *On the Horizon*, 9(5): 1–6.

Prensky, M. (2005) Listen to the natives, *Educational Leadership*, 63(4): 8–13.

Prosser, M. and Trigwell, K. (1999) *Understanding Learning and Teaching: The Experience in Higher Education.* Buckingham: Open University Press and Society for Research into Higher Education.

Quality Assurance Agency for Higher Education (QAA: http://www.qaa.ac.uk/academicinfrastructure/progressFiles/default.asp).

Ramsden, P. (1992) *Learning to Teach in Higher Education.* London: Routledge.

Rhodes, G. and Slaughter, S. (2006) Mode 3. Academic capitalism and the new economy: making higher education work for whom?, in P. Tynjala, J. Valimaa and G. Boulton-Lewis (eds) *Higher Education and Working Life: Collaborations, Confrontations and Challenges.* Amsterdam: Elsevier in association with Earli.

Rowntree, D. (1982) *Educational Technology in Curriculum Development.* London: Harper and Row.

Saljo, R. (1979) Learning about learning, *Higher Education,* 8: 443–51.

Samuelowicz, K. and Bain, J. D. (2001) Revisiting academics' beliefs about teaching and learning, *Higher Education,* 41: 299–325.

Scottish Executive (2003a) *Life Through learning: Learning Through Life.* www.scotland.gov.uk/Topics/Education/Life-Long-Learning/17722/9678

Scottish Executive (2003b) *A Partnership for a Better Scotland.* www. scotland.gov.uk/library5/ lifelong/llsm-00.asp

Searle, R. H. (2005) *Selection and Recruitment.* Buckingham: The Open University.

Seidman, A. (2006) *College Retention: Formula for Student Success.* Westport, CT: American Council on Education and Praeger Publishers.

Sinclair, C. (2006) *Understanding University: A Guide to Another Planet.* Buckingham: Open University Press.

Soros, G. (2008) *The New Paradigm for Financial Markets: The Credit Crisis of 2008 and What It Means.* Chatham: Pubic Affairs.

Sparrow, P. R. (1997) *Organizational Competencies: Creating a Strategic Framework for Selection and Assessment,* in N. Anderson and P. Herriot, *International Handbook of Selection and Assessment.* Chichester: Wiley.

Steffe, L. P. and Gale, J. (1995) *Constructivism in Education.* New York: Lawrence Erlbaum Associates.

Stenhouse, L. (1975) *An Introduction to Curriculum Research and Development.* London: Heinemann.

Stewart, J. and Knowles, V. (2000) Graduate recruitment and selection: implications for HE, graduates and small business recruiters, *Career Development International,* 5(2): 65–80.

Symes, C. and McIntyre, J. (eds) (2000) *Working Knowledge: The New Vocationalism and Higher Education.* Buckingham: Open University Press/Society for Research into Higher Education.

Tapscott, D. (1999) Educating the net generation, *Educational Leadership,* 56(5): 6–11.

Taylor, R., Barr, J. and Steele, T. (2002) *For a Radical Higher Education After Postmodernism.* Buckingham: Open University Press/ Society for Research into Higher Education.

Teichler, U. (1999) Higher education policy and the world of work: changing conditions and challenges, *Higher Education Policy,* 12: 285–312.

Thompson, P. and Warhurst, C. (1998) *Workplaces of the Future.* London: Palgrave Macmillan.

Tinto, V. (1975) Dropouts from higher education: a theoretical synthesis of the recent literature, *A Review of Educational Research*, 45: 89–125.

Tinto, V. (1989) Dropout from higher education: a theoretical synthesis of recent research, *Review of Educational Research*, 45 (1): 89–125.

Tinto, V. (1993) *Leaving College: Rethinking the Causes and Cures of Student Attrition*, 2nd edn. Chicago, IL: University of Chicago Press.

Tinto, V. (1997) Classrooms as communities: exploring the educational characteristics of student persistence, *Journal of Higher Education*, 68(6): 599–623.

Tinto, V. (2005) Epilogue: moving from theory to action, in A. Seidman, *College Retention: Formula for Student Success*. Westport, CT: American Council on Education and Praeger Publishers.

Tinto, V., Love, G. and Russo, P. (1994) *Building Learning Communities for New College Students*. Philadelphia, PA: Pennsylvania State University, National Centre on Post-secondary Teaching, Learning and Assessment.

Trow, M. (1974) Problems in the transition from elite to mass higher education, in OECD, *Policies for Higher Education*. General Report, Conference on Future Structures of Post-Secondary Education. Paris: OECD.

Warhurst, C., Grugulis, I. and Keep, E. (2004) *The Skills That Matter*. London: Palgrave.

Webber, S. and Johnston, B. (2005) Information literacy in the curriculum: selected findings from a phenomenographic study of UK academic's conceptions of, and pedagogy for, information literacy, in: C. Rust (ed.) *Improving Student Learning: Diversity and Inclusivity: Proceedings of the 11th ISL symposium, Birmingham, 6–8 September 2004*. Oxford: Oxford Brookes University.

Wheeler, S. and Birtles, J. (1993) *A Handbook for Personal Tutors*. Buckingham: Open University Press/Society for Research into Higher Education.

Whittaker, R. (2008) QAA First Year Enhancement Theme. Project 9 Final Report: Transition to and during the First Year. Glasgow: QAA.

Wimshurst, K. and Allard, T. (2008) Personal and institutional characteristics of student failure. *Assessment and Evaluation in Higher Education*. 33(6): 687–98.

Wingate, U. (2007) A framework for transition: supporting 'learning to learn' in higher education, *Higher Education Quarterly*, 61(3): 391–405.

Wolf, A. (2002) *Does Education Matter? Myths about Education and Economic Growth*. London: Penguin Books.

Yorke, M. (1999) *Leaving early: Undergraduate Non-completion in Higher Education*. London: Falmer Press.

Yorke, M. and Longden, B. (2004) *Retention and Student Success in Higher Education*. Maidenhead: Open University Press/Society for Research into Higher Education.

Yorke, M. and Longden, B. (2007) *The First-year Experience in Higher Education in the UK*. Report on Phase 1 of a project funded by the Higher Education Academy. www.heacademy.ac.uk/assets/York/documents/ourwork/research/FYE/web0573_the_first_year_experience.pdf

Yorke, M. and Longden, B. (2008) *The First-year Experience in Higher Education in the UK*. Final report for the Higher Education Academy. www.heacademy.ac.uk/assets/York/documents/ourwork/research/surveys/FYE/FYEFinalReport.pdf

Zepke, N., Leach, L. and Prebble, T. (2006) Being learner centred: one way to improve retention?, *Studies in Higher Education*, 31(5): 587–600.

Zukas, M. and Malcolm, J. (2007) Learning from adult education, *Academy Exchange*, (5) Summer: 21–2.

Index

FACILITATING REFLECTIVE LEARNING IN HIGHER EDUCATION

Second Edition

Anne Brockbank and Ian McGill

Praise for the previous edition:

"This is a passionate and practical book"

Teaching in Higher Education

"This book offers valuable insights into a process for becoming a reflective learner and for developing students into reflective learners as well."

Studies in Higher Education

This significantly revised edition includes the most current thinking on reflective learning as well as stories from academics and students that bring to life the practical impact of reflection in action. Based on sound theoretical concepts, the authors offer a range of solutions for different teaching situations, taking into account factors such as group size, physical space, and technology. They also offer facilitation rather than traditional teaching methods as a productive and useful skill that helps teachers and encourages students to interact and develop reflexive skills that can be used beyond their student years.

Based on rigorous theories, *Facilitating Reflective Learning in Higher Education* offers new insights for university and college teachers seeking to enhance or diversify their practices and allows them to effectively facilitate their students' reflective learning.

Contents: *Acknowledgements to second edition – Acknowledgements to first edition – **Part I Learning and reflection** – Our themes – Learning philosophies and principles – What is learning? A review of learning theories – Requirements for reflection – Reflection and reflective practice – **Part II Facilitating learning and reflective practice** – Academic practice and learning – Methods of reflection for tutors – Methods and assessment of reflective learning – Becoming a facilitator: Enabling reflective learning – Facilitation in practice: Basic skills – Facilitation in practice: Further skills – **Part III Exemplars** – Action learning (learning sets) – Academic supervision – Mentoring – Conclusion.*

2007   192pp

978-0-335-22091-5 (Paperback)   978-0-335-22092-2 (Hardback)

ENHANCING LEARNING, TEACHING, ASSESSMENT AND CURRICULUM IN HIGHER EDUCATION

Veronica Bamber, Paul Trowler, Murray Saunders and Peter Knight

Higher education is a particularly complex site for enhancement initiatives. This book offers those involved in change a coherent conceptual overview of enhancement approaches, of the change context, and of the probable interactions between them.

The book sets enhancement within a particular type of change dynamic which focuses on social practices. The aim is to base innovation and change on the probabilities of desired outcomes materializing, rather than on the romanticism of policies that underestimate the sheer difficulty of making a difference. Following a theoretical introduction to these ideas, there are case studies (from the UK, Australia, New Zealand, South Africa and Norway) at the national, institutional, departmental and individual levels, illustrating the argument that enhancement is best achieved when it works with social practices in real institutional and organizational settings.

In a final section, the authors link the case examples and theoretical frameworks, inviting readers to consider their own enhancement situations and apply the 'frameworks for action' offered in earlier sections of the book.

The book doesn't offer quick-fix solutions but aims to support change with practical examples, conceptual tools and reflexive questions for those involved in change at all levels. It is key reading for higher education lecturers, managers, educational developers and policy makers.

Contents – Preface by Dr Liz Beaty Introduction: Continuities, enhancement and higher education – Enhancement theories – Theme 1: Influencing the disciplines – Introduction – Changing the rules of engagement – Layers of the onion – Talking the talk, walking the walk – Against the grain – Commentary – Theme 2: The Scottish way – Up and down the implementation staircase – Carrots but no sticks – PASS the word – Exchange and art – Commentary – Theme 3: Developing frameworks for action – Introduction – Strong vision, low prescription – Can we teach higher education management? – Changing learning architectures, shifting practices – Bringing new learning to old cultures – Commentary – Theme 4: Challenging practices in learning, teaching, assessment and curriculum – Introduction – Contesting discourses in higher education curricula – Academic development as changing social practice – Frustrated aspirations – Freedom to innovate, freedom to resist – Commentary – Making practical sense of enhancing learning, teaching, assessment and curriculum – References- Index

2009   224pp
978-0-335-23375-5 (Paperback)   978-0-335-23376-2 (Hardback)

THE SCHOLARSHIP OF TEACHING AND LEARNING IN HIGHER EDUCATION

Rowena Murray (ed)

This book is designed for lecturers on a wide range of professional courses. It directly addresses questions that come up again and again in seminar discussions; questions that are fundamental to the values and perspectives of academics across the disciplines:

- What is meant by the scholarship of teaching and learning in higher education?
- What is the purpose of higher education?
- Are lecturers really 'students' on these courses?
- How do you do 'reflective' writing?
- What do we do with all this theory and jargon?
- What does CPD in this area involve?
- How do you do 'research' on teaching and learning?

This book does not treat each element of the curriculum separately – course design, assessment, evaluation of teaching etc. – since that approach has been well handled by others. Instead, like other books in the series, it addresses elements of the curriculum in an integrated way, thereby educating the reader in how to approach a range of higher education related issues.

is book provides a scholarly introduction to the literature on these questions. Like other books in the series, it offers a concise treatment of complex questions. It also provides directions for future study.

Contents – List of contributors – Introduction – The scholarship of teaching and learning in higher education: an overview – What's learning for?- Lecturers as students – Learning to write about teaching – Resources on higher education teaching and learning – Starting with the discipline – Beyond common sense – Evaluating teaching and learning – Reconsidering scholarship reconsidered – Doing small-scale qualitative research on educational innovation- Index

2008 168pp

978-0-335-23446-2 (Paperback)

978-0-335-23445-5 (Hardback)